D0861546

Feb. 27, 2008

I Love You
Maries.
The boy

BIBLE DAY BY DAY

"Blessed is the person who . . . delights in the law of the Lord and meditates on His law day and night" (Ps 1:1-2).

Bible Day by Day

MINUTE MEDITATIONS
FOR EVERY DAY
BASED ON SELECTED TEXTS
OF THE HOLY BIBLE

By
Rev. John C. Kersten, S.V.D.

Illustrated

CATHOLIC BOOK PUBLISHING CORP.
New York

CONTENTS

NIHIL OBSTAT: John J. Quinn, M.A.
Censor Librorum

IMPRIMATUR: ✠ Patrick J. Sheridan, D.D.
Vicar General, Archdiocese of New York

(T-150)

PRAYER BEFORE READING
SACRED SCRIPTURE

Come, Holy Spirit,
fill the hearts of Your faithful
and enkindle in them the fire of Your love.

℣. Send forth Your Spirit and they shall be
created.

℟. And You shall renew the face of the earth.

Let us pray.
O God, You instructed the hearts of the faithful
by the light of the Holy Spirit.
Grant us by the same Holy Spirit
to have a right judgment in all things
and ever to rejoice in His consolation.

PRAYER AFTER READING
SACRED SCRIPTURE

Let me not,
O Lord,
be puffed up with worldly wisdom,
which passes away.
Grant me that love which never abates,
that I may not choose to know anything among
   human beings
but Jesus and Him crucified.

I pray You, loving Jesus,
that as You have graciously given me
to drink in with delight the words of Your knowledge,
so You would mercifully grant me
to attain one day to You,
the Fountain of all wisdom,
and to appear forever before Your face.

PREFACE

"How I love Your law, O Lord! It is my meditation all the day. . . . Your word is a lamp to my feet and a light to my path" (Ps 119:97, 105).

This is a pocket meditation book for busy people. In writing my comments, I have tried to avoid the pitfall of having the reader meditate on my words rather than on the word of God as quoted from the Bible. Please take my brief remarks as a starting point for meditative prayer on the Bible text itself, and whenever you have more time turn for meditation to your complete Bible. Make time and arrange a quiet place for concentration in accord with Jesus' invitation: "Come apart to a deserted place and rest a while" (Mk 6:31).

In composing these notes, it was my intention to keep Christianity as lived in the Catholic tradition credible to historically minded intellectuals. Prayerful bible reading must go hand in hand with sound Biblical scholarship, which, of course, submits its findings to the teaching authority (Magisterium) of the Church (see *Dogmatic Constitution on Divine Revelation*, nos. 12, 23). Fundamentalism, literalism and naive disregard of historical facts undermine faith in both the Scriptures and the Institutional Church.

If you are a Christian with questions concerning your faith in both the Scriptures and the Church, give this book a try! Questions do exist. We should not dodge them. Keep in mind, though, that you must handle faith as you do love. they are akin and can survive only if dealt with in the right way. Intellectual Catholics who struggle with doubts and questions often overlook this important point.

Every year, I receive a number of Christmas cards with only a signature on them. The wish on the card was composed by somebody other than the sender. My question: Did the sender even read that wish? I prefer a personal Christmas wish. The wording may be less perfect, but it indicates that the writer has been thinking of me for at least a short moment. When composing these meditations, I was encouraged to add a prayer after each of them. This seemed to me to be the same as sending a Christmas card with a signature only.

I have followed a middle of the road solution. Sometimes I add a prayer. Every so often I suggest praying. Often I don't. But by all means never do your reflective Bible reading without a prayer that spontaneously sprouts from it. If you fail to do so, you are wasting your time!

John C. Kersten, S.V.D.

ANITY of vanities. All things are vanity! What profit does a man have from all the labor at which he toils —Eccl 1:1-2

JAN. 1

Jesus Our Wisdom

King Solomon had everything he could dream of, yet he states: "A thankless task has God laid on men to be busied about" (Eccl 1:13). Is life just a "thankless task"? Jesus, greater than Solomon (Mt 12:42), says: "Come to Me, all you who labor and are burdened . . . and I will give you rest." (Mt 11:28-29).

We Christians learn how to handle life from God's wisdom wherever found—but most of all as incarnated in the Lord Jesus.

SAID in my heart, "Come, let me test you with pleasure and the enjoyment of good things. . . ." Behold! all was meaningless and a chasing after the wind.

JAN. 2

—Eccl 2:1, 3, 10, 11

Lasting Satisfaction

A similar message is suggested when we sit through the TV commercials. Only the last part is omitted. When you are still young, you will be easily fascinated. But do you have to be old in order to be wise? Listening to Jesus teaching in the synagogue of Nazareth, people asked: "What is this wisdom that has been given Him?" (Mk 6:2). Jesus was in His early thirties!

He says: "Blessed are they who hunger and thirst for justice, for they will be satisfied" (Mt 5:6). Only lasting satisfaction gives peace and consequently happiness.

9

ISDOM has excelled over folly as much as light differs from darkness. . . . How is it that the wise man dies! —Eccl 2:13, 16

Christian Wisdom

Christian wisdom has us live with the tension between "making the best of life now" and "faith in the life to come." We know about the two sparrows not falling to the ground without our Father's knowledge and Jesus' comforting words: "Do not be afraid; you are of more value than many sparrows" (Mt 10:31).

When it gets dark around me, I find light, guidance, and protection by prayerfully turning to my heavenly Father.

 N the place of judgment I saw wickedness, and in the place of justice, wickedness. . . . And I have found that nothing is better for a man than to rejoice in his work.

—Eccl 3:16, 22

Faith Overcomes Human Imperfections

I see human imperfections even in my Church from the Vatican down to the hall where my parish council is meeting. Jesus spoke His "woes" on the religious leaders of His time, but He also said: "Observe and do all things that they command you" (Mt 23:3).

Whatever the media may say about the Pope, bishops, priests, and theologians, and regardless of the situation in your own congregation, strive to remain dedicated to Christ and what He stands for and "rejoice in your work!"

REMEMBER your Creator in the days of your youth, before the time of affliction comes and the years draw near of which you will say, They please me not. —Eccl 12:1

Moved by Love Not Calculation

A motive for remembering your Maker all your life may be well understood self-interest. Ruling out infidelity, a man said: "I don't want to jeopardize what I have [family]." His wife would agree: "He better not," but would she appreciate such a calculating attitude?

God is your lover. "Whoever does not love does not know God; for God is love" (1 Jn 4:8). Outgrowing calculation, I should be motivated by love ever more.

WHERE can wisdom be found, and where is the place of understanding? —Job 28:12

The Mystery of Evil

Job is down in the dumps. He has lost everything. We can understand his mood: "Let the day perish on which I was born" (Job 3:3). We may be in a mood like Job's. We may look for an answer. God is a loving Father. Why then all the pain in the world: my own problems, those of my family and friends, hunger and suffering abroad as I see it on TV? A mystery!

As for wisdom, insight, and understanding, in faith we follow "all the Scriptures" (Lk 24:27). "God knows the way to it [wisdom]; and He alone knows its dwelling" (Job 28:23).

HAT people may appreciate wisdom and discipline, may understand words of insight; may be trained in wise conduct, doing what is right and just and fair. —Prov 1:2-3

A Good Life

For us to be honest requires self-discipline and training. My paycheck shall stand for a job well done.

"Who among you is wise and understanding? Let him by a good life show his works in the meekness that derives from wisdom" (Jas 3:13). James refers to a wisdom from above. Self-discipline and training are required to get this wisdom from above, but so is prayer.

———

 Y son, heed your father's instruction, and forsake not your mother's teaching. They will be a garland to grace your head. —Prov 1:8-9

Gratitude toward Parents

As an adult, how do you relate to your parents? Obedience is not a binding requirement any longer, but the duty of love and respect remains. In their time our parents did what they considered right. Are we grateful?

How often do you spend time with your parents and listen to them? Do you write or call them regularly? Parishioners ask quite often that the Sunday Liturgy be celebrated in loving memory of their parents. It is a way of keeping alive their memory. The Lord asked us to celebrate in memory of Him!

T is the Lord Who gives wisdom; out of His mouth come knowledge and understanding.

—Prov 2:6

JAN.
9

Two Kinds of Wisdom

James mentions two kinds of wisdom. One is earthly, unspiritual, and demonic and is qualified by jealousy, selfish ambition, disorder, and foul practice (Jas 3:14-16). It can ruin families, church life, and careers.

The other wisdom comes from above. It is pure, peaceable, gentle, compliant, full of mercy and good fruits, without inconstancy or insincerity (Jas 3:17). Since this wisdom comes from the mouth of God, we should search for it in our Bible and humbly ask for it in prayer.

———————

E not wise in your own eyes . . . keep sound judgment and discernment in view. . . . Then you will go on your way safely; your foot will never stumble.

—Prov 3:7, 21, 23

JAN.
10

Seeking Good Counsel

When tedium, ennui, conflict of opinion, hurt feelings and consequently alienation enter your marriage, is your first option a call to the lawyer or rather to a friend or counselor, who is willing and able to help? When your body is hurting, you hasten to your physician. What about your more or less sick relationship as spouses? Books and cassettes issued by professional marriage counselors are available.

And if single, you may need advice as well. Face to face confession could be an option!

ISDOM is supreme: therefore, get wisdom; at the cost of all you have, get understanding.

—Prov 4:7

Real Wisdom Comes from God

In order to do anything, you must find it precious, especially when you want it at the cost of all you have. Is wisdom and understanding that precious to you? We know how stupid people can ruin their lives.

Paul mentions people who lost "wisdom" and became vain in their reasoning with their senseless minds darkened. While claiming to be wise, they became fools (Rom 1:21, 22, 30, 31). We too may lose track if we do not persevere in our search for real wisdom, which comes from God.

E who loves discipline loves knowledge, but he who hates correction is stupid.

—Prov 12:1

Accepting Correction

As a child, I had to take correction and reproof from my parents. As a student, I had to take tests, and the returns were not always flattering. As an adult, am I willing to accept corrective remarks?

In faith do I listen to the Sunday sermon, even if the preacher is not as eloquent as many a televangelist? I should pay attention to what is said and how it applies to me (not to my neighbor in church!) even when the message is not gift-wrapped in fancy paper with a red ribbon on top.

A N anxious heart weighs a man down, but a kind word makes him glad.

—Prov 12:25

JAN.
13

A Kind Word

A supervisor gave an extended lunch break to a worker to visit a sick wife. The result was a happy smile on the worker's face and better work done in the afternoon! Good business! Am I aware that a kind word to a depressed coworker may lead to a similar miracle?

You might say, "I have my own problems. Let each take care of his own." But did you ever have the experience that alleviating someone else's sorrow, speaking that kind word, made it easier to carry your own burden? It is the wisdom of sharing.

L IKE a city whose defenses are broken down is the man [or woman] with no check on his [or her] feelings.

—Prov 25:28

JAN.
14

The Proper Use of Feelings

Not feeling like getting up in time causes rush-hour accidents on Monday morning. Not feeling like swallowing blood pressure pills causes confinement to wheelchairs and premature deaths. Not feeling like changing the habit of jealousy and gossiping may hurt another's feelings, and hurt feelings are often chain reactions of much grief.

Feelings are good, but if you don't check them and have the intellect and will step in, you will be hurt and do harm to others. You are defenseless.

HE speaks with wisdom, and on her tongue is faithful instruction.

—Prov 31:26

Living Is Relating

Relationship in both the nuclear family and the extended one (friends, coworkers, parishioners), must be based on growing knowledge of one another, appreciation, mutual respect, and love, hence founded on real values. "Charm is deceptive and beauty is fleeting" (Prov 31:30).

How do I develop my relationships? Am I growing as a loving person, so that others can relate to me in respect and love? And do I relate to them not because of "fleeting beauty" but because they are beautiful persons?

 OVE is as strong as death, and devotion is as unyielding as the netherworld; it burns like a blazing fire.

—SS 8:6

Love is as Strong as Death

The obvious meaning of the Song of Songs is love between man and woman. Of course, the portrayal is conditioned by time and culture. Spouses can learn from it, and so can singles—since love is a universal value.

What is your concept of love? Do the notions "strong" (firm and uncompromising), "unyielding" (determined as to fidelity?) and "blazing fire" (fully alive by using all the means that nature and grace afford!) fit into it? A marriage does not necessarily have to get stale because of age!

BELONG to my lover and He yearns for me." —SS 7:10

We Belong to God

The Judeo-Christian tradition sees the Song of Songs as a parable, describing the mutual love of the Lord and His people in terms of human love. The true meaning of mutual love comes from the poem as a whole.

How do you feel related to God? Isaiah writes, "For your Maker has become your husband" (Isa 54:5). The notions of punishment and reward may enter the picture. The Bible uses these motives as parents do with children! We should outgrow fear and the want of gain. You could meditate on the value "belonging" vs. "loneliness." God yearns for you.

HE souls of the just are in the hand of God, and no torment can overtake them. —Wis 3:1

Consolation in Time of Death

All of us have to face the departure of a dearly beloved every so often. How do we handle it? Indeed, "from the viewpoint of the foolish they seemed to be dead . . . . But they are at peace" (Wis 3:23).

Since there is no scientific proof of a hereafter, in faith we turn to God's word in Scripture. At the funeral service, we look at the lighted Easter candle, symbol of the risen Lord, Whom we hope to follow into life everlasting, and consolation is found in common prayer.

THEY journeyed through an inhospitable desert. . . . When they were thirsty they cried out to you, and water was given them out of unyielding rock. —Wis 11:2-4

God—Able and Willing to Help

In time of need to whom do we turn? Isn't it to someone who we know is able and willing to help? My late brother James was a capable man and always ready to help free of charge.

From history the Hebrews knew that God was able and willing to help. Hence, they turned to Him whenever they were in need. To whom do you turn when in need, especially when human resources are exhausted?

UT You, our God, are good and faithful, slow to anger, and showing mercy in governing the universe. Even if we sin, we are Yours, for we acknowledge Your power. —Wis 15:1-2

Sin and Forgiveness

On the human level, are you aware that you hurt the feelings of others every so often? When you happen to do so, do you apologize? If others have wronged you, can you forgive?

Only if you have apologized and forgiven can you believe in the possibility of sin. Our relationship with God is one of mutual love. That's why possibly we sin more by negligence than by malice. Aware of God's mercy, turn to Him whenever you are guilty of omission or carelessness.

A LL wisdom derives from the Lord and remains with Him forever.

—Sir 1:1

JAN. 21

All Wisdom Is from God

The pessimist, who looks at the gloomy side of things, is narrowminded. The mystery of evil will always be with us, but so will the wisdom that is with God! And He still pours it forth upon all His works, upon every living thing according to His bounty (Sir 1:8).

Do you see God's wisdom in a newborn baby or in the eyes of your spouse? Are you grateful when you have made a right decision? Even human wisdom, properly understood, comes from God! Do you experience God's wisdom during a brisk walk in nature? There is wisdom in taking a daily walk and meditating during it.

B E like a father to the fatherless, and act like a husband to their mother.

—Sir 4:10

JAN. 22

True Social Concern

A black priest in Chicago is concerned about the numbers of fatherless children who roam the streets. He himself has adopted two boys, and he encourages couples to do the same.

All Christians should be socially concerned somehow. Perhaps your parish is involved in projects of this nature. Real love and concern will show the way. Sirach promises, "You will then be like a child of the Most High, and His love for you will be greater than that of your own mother" (Sir 4:10).

19

O not be so confident of pardon that you add sin upon sin. Do not say, "His mercy is great; He will forgive my many sins." —Sir 5:5-6

A Meaningful Life

One sin, which even God cannot undo, is the sin of omission, a wasted life. If you have failed to make your life meaningful by doing good, you will be dissatisfied regardless of whether God forgives you or not.

Your life, though, is meaningful as long as in each situation you ask what the most loving thing to do is and try to do it.

 E quick to listen, but deliberate in offering your answer. The tongue can be the cause of its owner's downfall. —Sir 5:13, 15

Moderation in Speech

A Roman contemporary of Sirach states, "If you had kept your mouth shut, you would have remained a sage!" Running one's mouth is still a beloved pastime. Making a fool of oneself goes with it.

Looking at both sides of the coin requires wisdom and patience. What is your approach? "Innocent till proven guilty" reflects the wisdom of our Founding Fathers. "Examine first, and then criticize!" (Sir 11:7). Prayerfully say, "I will watch my ways and keep my tongue from sin" (Ps 39:2).

FAITHFUL friend is a strong defense; anyone who finds one possesses a treasure. —Sir 6:14

JAN. 25

Value of Faithful Friends

For married people, the faithful friend spoken of by Sirach is first of all the spouse. But besides the nuclear family we need an extended family made up of friends and relatives. The prophet Elisha had friends (2 Ki 4:8-37), and so did the Lord Jesus (Jn 11:5; 15:15-17). Sirach calls a faithful friend a life-saving medicine (6:16).

Especially in diaspora situations we need faithful Catholic friends without being exclusive. And the best way to keep friends is to be a good friend yourself!

F you are willing to listen, you will learn; and if you pay attention, you will become wise. —Sir 6:33

JAN. 26

The Art of Listening

We are all acquainted with the compulsive talker who gives nobody the opportunity to finish a sentence. In the company of equals, he/she is a nuisance, but we can walk away. At a sickbed, he/she is a poor visitor with the patient a captive audience. If he/she is your superior, you listen but have your thoughts.

Do you ever visit a nursing home? Listening requires a certain degree of humility and patience. Both are Christian virtues that reflect wisdom and should be asked for in prayer.

EFLECT on the decrees of the Lord and constantly meditate on His commandments. —Sir 6:37

Meditating on God's Word

Prayerfully meditating and reflecting on God's word is not typical of Christians in the Catholic tradition. The present book may help you to meditate as Sirach suggests it be done.

Even when you do your meditating on the commuter train, you must quiet down and concentrate. A quiet corner in your home, where there is no TV, radio, or noise, serves the purpose better! Thank God for His word to us in the Bible!

 UMBLE yourself to the greatest possible degree, for the godless will suffer the punishment of fire and worms. —Sir 7:17

Humility before God

Each of us wants and needs to be a somebody. Burdened with an inferiority complex, the oversensitive person is miserable and fails in life. Being a somebody, achieving a few things, and growing in self-confidence are good pursuits. However, when we sever our activities from God, they are nothing but "pride to be humbled!"

Sirach states, "The beginning of man's pride is to withdraw his heart from his Maker" (10:12). The moment you forget your total dependence on God, you are infected with a pride that the Bible condemns.

FEAR the Lord and honor the priest, and give him his portion as you have been commanded. —Sir 7:31

Honoring God and the Church

Thirty-four times the Bible mentions the duty of "tithing" on behalf of the sanctuary. More important than contributions, however, are the honor and respect we owe to God and the priest, human as he may be.

Honoring God is a divine law; doing it together every Sunday is a wise law of the Church. We need our mutual inspiration; hence each of us is responsible for a meaningful Liturgy on Sunday. Check your attitude!

DO not neglect to visit the sick, for as a result of such deeds you will be loved. —Sir 7:35

Visiting the Sick

We readily follow Sirach's advice to visit the sick when it concerns close relatives. But our Christian concern should go over and beyond our own family. In our well organized society, the physical needs of the sick are taken care of fairly well. But the need for company, consolation, and encouragement is left unfilled.

Why not ask the social worker in your local nursing home for the names of some the most neglected and lonesome people and adopt them? Then visit them with one of your friends.

THE heart changes one's countenance either for good or for evil.
—Sir 13:25

Genuine Goodheartedness

Actors can laugh and cry on command. They are trained for it. In the family, be it the nuclear or the extended one of relatives and friends, we should not act. Our smile should be a sign of a good heart. We should focus on goodness of heart as the source of our kindness.

The good-hearted person sees goodness all around; the evil-hearted person, evil. Do I try to be positive in my thinking of others? Is my "cheerful countenance" a sign of my real self?

AFOOL who has heard something suffers birth pangs like a woman in labor with a child.
—Sir 19:10

The Evil of Gossip

Is Sirach a male chauvinist? He was conditioned, of course, by his male oriented culture, just as we are part of our own time and stage of civilization. But Sirach personifies wisdom as a woman and does not describe only women as traditional gossipers! Both males and females can be afflicted.

Gossip has done more harm than the worst disease can do to the human race. Male or female, check your conversation habits. Can you suspend your opinion till you have seen the other side of the coin?

CAME forth from the mouth of the Most High and covered the earth like a mist. . . . I became established in Zion.

FEB. 2

— Sir 24:1, 3, 10

God's Wisdom Given Us

God's wisdom is involved in all of creation. In Zion Israel, though, God's wisdom "fixed [her] abode" in a special way. The Bible reflects that wisdom. Coming forth from God's mouth, it is a word spoken to you and me.

"With the learned be conversant" (Sir 9:15). Who is more learned than Almighty God? For guidance and light we turn to Him in Scripture, without overlooking wisdom wherever found in nature or in fellow human beings.

 HE creator of all things gave me [Wisdom] His command, . . . saying, "Make your dwelling in Jacob."

FEB. 3

— Sir 24:8

God's Wisdom-Word-Light

Figuratively personified, God's wisdom is found in Israel, its preachers, and its Scriptures (the Old Testament). However, we see God's wisdom-word-light incarnated and dwelling in the Lord Jesus in such a way that the New Testament calls Him "Son of God" (Jn 1:14). Consequently, Jesus was aware of God as His Father (Lk 11:2).

And we who accept Him are children of God as well (Jn 1:12). Hence, we may share that awareness. Accepting the Lord Jesus is a lifelong process.

25

HE prayer of the humble pierces the clouds; it does not rest until it reaches the Lord. — Sir 35:17

Prayer of Trust

When at night, storm, thunder, lightning, and dark clouds were frightening us, my parents lighted a blessed candle and we prayed the rosary. Some may see this as superstition of a past era. No matter. The prayer of these "humble" people pierced those dark clouds.

My parents possessed an unsophisticated faith and hope that I sometimes envy. They believed in their "way." "Hear, O Lord, the prayer of Your servants, according to Your goodwill toward Your people" (Sir 36:16). How is your prayer in your "way" right now?

 AVE pity on us, Master, Lord of the universe. —Sir 36:1

Prayer of Petition

Prayer of petition makes sense only if we feel dependent on a higher reality experienced as God, Maker, Provider, and Father. We should feel "humble" (Sir 35:17). When monks celebrate the Divine Office, they start by singing, "God, come to our assistance," because "we do not know how to pray as we ought" (Rom 8:26). God must help me to get up from my lowliness and direct heart and mind to him.

Prayer itself is a gift. Especially when you don't feel like praying, ask and "the Spirit [will come] to help our weakness" (Rom 8:26).

MY child, see what suits your constitution . . . and do not be greedy for food. —Sir 37:26-29

Christian Temperance

The media are slowly changing the eating habits of Americans. We have been eating too much and consequently dying prematurely of heart attacks and strokes.

A century before Christ, Sirach stated, "For overeating leads to illness, and gluttony brings on nausea. Many have died as a result of gluttony, but the one who guards against it prolongs his life" (Sir 37:29-30). Health care, cleanliness, reasonable eating and drinking habits are Christian virtues in the perspective of faithful stewardship to my Maker.

———

LET us now praise illustrious men, our ancestors in their successive generations. —Sir 44:1

Honoring the Saints

Keeping alive the memory of great men and women means keeping alive their ideals. And we need ideals to pursue. Without them life becomes stale and boring. We maintain statues of great Americans. On Memorial Day, we ponder their great deeds, honor them, and decide to follow their example.

We Christians also honor our Saints. Their statues and memorial days keep their memory alive. We try to follow their example. Who are your favorite Saints?

AGNIFY the Lord with me, let us extol His name together.

— Ps 34:4

Praying in Common

Praying together during time of grief, is something we Christians in the Catholic tradition must learn again. Turning to our heavenly Father together creates the feeling of belonging that all of us need. We pray for our deceased. As much as this sort of prayer helps them, it benefits us who stay behind and must continue our journey through this valley of tears.

There is great wisdom in the Church's insistence that her members pray and worship together every Sunday.

ITH those who take advice is wisdom.   — Prov 13:10

Prayerful Confession

We should think carefully about making every so often a face-to-face Confession (Confession with prayerful dialogue)—at a time when both confessor-counselor and penitent-counselee are not in a hurry.

Sharing guilt and being assured that a merciful Father understands and forgives is beneficial. Moreover, the search for growing in love needs guidance. Do you want to grow as a Christian without being afraid to change a few habits if "prayerful dialogue" points in that direction? Pray to the Holy Spirit, Who often operates through fellow human beings.

OTHING is better than fear of the Lord.

—Sir 23:27

FEB.
10

Filial Respect for God

In Biblical idiom, fear of the Lord means "filial respect for God." It is a cherished value of Sirach. It warms the heart (1:10); it is the beginning of wisdom (1:12); it surpasses all else (25:11); it is a paradise of blessings (40:27); nothing is better! "Blessed is the man who devotes himself to these things. . . . If he puts them into practice, he will be able to cope with anything, for fear of [filial respect for] the Lord is his lamp" (50:28-29).

What light are you going by: the candlelight many are using or the radiance of the Lord?

 NOTHER is slow and in need of help, lacking in strength and abounding in poverty. — Sir 11:12

FEB.
11

The Measure of Greatness

Not everyone can be a George Washington or an Albert Einstein. But the life of every person who does the loving thing in his/her situation is meaningful. A mother spending time with her children, a father listening to his son, a student doing his homework—all are great in the eyes of God. The person who cares only for satisfying his/her self is a failure.

Every Sunday we pray, "I confess to Almighty God . . . that I have sinned . . . in what I have failed to do." Real repentance should result in trying to do the most loving thing!

URSED be the gossipers and the double-tongued, for they destroy the lives of many. —Sir 28:13

Thinking Positive

There is a legend that the Lord's disciples once saw a dead and partly decomposed dog. They remarked, "It stinks!" The Lord Jesus said, "Look at how beautiful its teeth are!"

Our thinking about other human beings comes to the fore in our speech. When you meet a person for the first time you get an impression. Do you blurt it out right away? Are you concerned not to destroy the peace in your community? The remedy for the gossip-addict is to change from negative to positive thinking and to pray for God's help.

 FAITHFUL friend is beyond price; there is no possible way to measure his worth. —Sir 6:15

True Friendship

It is important to choose right friends. "When you wish to aquire a new friend, first test him" (Sir 6:7). Youngsters should heed this advice. Why? "Anyone who associates with the proud will become like them" (Sir 13:1). This applies to both old and young! "A friend who will not stand by you in time of trouble" (Sir 6:10) is of no value.

Have you denied a friend a favor that you could easily have granted? Friendship requires love and going out of your way every so often.

OW different a situation it is with the man who devotes himself to the study of the law of the Most High.

FEB. 14

— Sir 39:1

Molded by God's Word

Prayerful study of the law of the Most High— the Bible—should make you different. For example, being judgmental, I should not see malice where the Lord Jesus sees ignorance: "Father, forgive them, for they know not what they do" (Lk 23:34). Am I open-minded enough to accept the message?

God will direct your knowledge and counsel, as you meditate upon His mysteries, "and the wisdom you desire will be granted" (Sir 6:37).

ONAH got ready to flee to Tarshish away from the face of the Lord.

FEB. 15

—Jon 1:2

Overcoming Frustration

We know the story of Jonah's call and his reluctance to go and preach in Nineveh. A large fish swallowed the prophet, and when finally it spewed poor Jonah upon the shore, who was waiting for him? The Lord, who told him a second time, "Go." Can I dodge my call in life without ruining myself?

When things don't go my way, I too may get frustrated like Jonah: "And now, Lord, I beg You, take my life from me!" (Jon 4:3). Getting frustrated is human. Pray for strength to overcome and to be faithful to your call.

I N the beginning God created the heavens and the earth.

—Gen 1:1

FEB.
16

God the Creator

Creationists, who teach that matter was created substantially as it now exists by the Creator, are battling evolutionists on how God actually created the universe. Both opinions can be held by Christians. However, creationists err in referring to the Bible as a book of science, which it is not. The Bible teaches that God created the universe not when and how.

Paul states, "In Him we live and move and have our being" (Acts 17:18). I should grow in my awareness of being in God.

G OD created human beings in His image, in the image of God He created them; male and female He created them. —Gen 1:27

FEB.
17

Living Up to God's Image

We resemble God primarily because of dominion that God gives us over the rest of creation (Ps 8:7).

As God's coworkers, we adults are responsible for what kind of people a subsequent generation will be. And since children go by images, we should be creatively involved by word and example. Environmentalists have a point. Both the litterbug and the person who gives a poor example to children are deficient coworkers of the Creator, not living up to God's image after which they were created.

GOD saw all that He had made, and behold, it was very good.

— Gen 1:31

The World's Goodness

The "mystery of iniquity," evil and frustrations, overwhelming us may create a negative outlook on life. Some people even give up, commit suicide, or turn to drugs and alcohol. But our starting point for contemplating life and the environment in which it is situated should be its goodness. "God saw . . . [that] it was very good" (Gen 1:31). No person is entirely evil.

Do I try to think positively even in the darkest of life's situations? It requires faith. The mystery of iniquity can be approached but not fully explained.

HE Lord God said, "It is not good for the man to be alone. I wish to make another creature who will be like him." — Gen 2:18

Divine-Human Partnership

The text cited above refers first of all to the marital relationship. Besides sex, there are many activities that enhance fellowship and love. Married people should be aware of the lifelong task to grow as suitable partners.

To be alone is not good for any person. All of us need friends and should keep friendship alive. Moreover, we need partnership with God, Who is love and wants to relate to us in love. Even the most ardent lover on the human level must go it alone sooner or later.

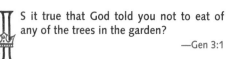

I S it true that God told you not to eat of any of the trees in the garden?

—Gen 3:1

FEB. 20

The Most Loving Thing to Do

One starting point of ethical thinking is "What is the law? What must one do or not do in order to avoid sin?" A more Christian starting point is "What is the most loving thing to do in each situation of one's life?"

The temptation to ask "Did God really tell me?" is obvious when the law is your starting point of thinking. Quite often you find a way out or do just the minimum required. However, "What is the most loving thing to do?" appeals constantly to our generosity.

G OD said to Noah . . . , "I will establish My covenant with you and your descendants after you."

— Gen 9:8

FEB. 21

Covenant—An agreement of Love

The Bible uses the concept of "covenant" 298 times to describe how it sees God relating to us and vice versa. Initially, covenant follows the pattern of any legal contract that desert sheikhs made with one another: "I will be your God-protector and you will serve me."

Later, "love" enters the picture ever more. Covenant becomes an agreement of love, and in the New Testament it is related to the blood of Christ (Lk 22:20). I should outgrow a legalistic relationship with God and let love prevail.

HE Lord said to Abram: "Leave your country, your people, and the house of your father, and go to the land to which I will lead you." —Gen 12:1

The Primacy of Faith

"Abram departed just as the Lord had ordered him" (Gen 12:4). Because of his faith, time and again Abraham is mentioned in the Bible. Paul writes, "[Abraham] believed, hoping against hope, that he would become 'the father of many nations.'. . . No distrust made him waiver concerning God's promise" (Rom 4:18, 20).

Following your call in life—be it marital, parental, religious, or single—can be done only with faith in self, fellow human beings, and God. Check all three relations.

ALK before Me and be blameless.

—Gen 17:1

Conversing with God

You can be locally present (e.g., in an overcrowded bus) and yet personally far away (e.g., bearing with a boring compulsive talker). What matters is a personal presence, the manner in which friends share their personalities. It is the way God wants us to walk in His presence.

Conversing with God, we should be as honest as lovers are supposed to be. How do you experience God? Daily meditation may enhance intimacy!

I S anything impossible to the Lord?
—Gen 18:14

FEB.
24

Trust in God amid Depression

God promises Sarah and Abraham a child in their old age. Sarah cannot help laughing. Yet she bore a son at the set time that God had stated (Gen 18:13; 21:2). Teaching in story form, the Bible tells us to have trust in God.

Psychologists say that the cause of depression is often a negative interpretation of events surrounding our lives. With the above words of God in mind, a Christian can overcome depression. Pray often: "To You, O Lord, I lift up my soul; in You I trust, O my God" (Ps 25:1-2).

T AKE your son . . . and offer him as a holocaust.
— Gen 22:2

FEB.
25

Obedience to the Will of God

The sacred author says that "God tested Abraham" (Gen 22:1), giving us an advantage that Abraham did not have. He did not know of the "test" and that the Lord's messenger would tell him not to lay his hand on the boy (Gen 22:11). The story pushes to a climax, Abraham's perfect obedience!

Guided by faith, we must find out what our Maker wants us to do (the most loving thing!) in each situation and try to follow Abraham's obedience. "Your will be done!" (Mt 6:10).

THEY [Joseph's brothers] said to one another: "Here comes the dreamer! Come, let us kill him." —Gen 37:19-20

FEB. 26

The Vice of Jealousy

Jacob loved Joseph best of all his sons, and this made his other sons jealous (Gen 37:3-4). Their jealousy resulted in violence.

Jealousy, disrupts both family life and church work. It makes offices and assembly lines hell. Envious resentment surfaces as vicious gossip, becomes hatred, and may even result in injustice and violence. We should pray, "Lord, make me an instrument of Your peace" and strive to be peacemakers.

JOSEPH said to them, "Do not fear. Am I God?"

—Gen 50:19

FEB. 27

Forgiveness of Others

Jacob's sons had been very nasty to their brother Joseph (Gen 37:25-36). After Jacob's death, they became fearful that Joseph would repay them in full for all the wrong they did him (Gen 50:15). When they expressed their fears, Joseph spoke kindly to them, thus reassuring them (Gen 50:21).

The Bible tells us to be as magnanimous as Joseph was. Let God make a final judgment while we pray: "Forgive us our trespasses as we forgive those who trespass against us."

PENING [the basket], [Pharaoh's daughter] looked, and behold, there was a baby boy crying! — Ex 2:6

FEB.
28

Precious in God's Eyes

The Bible often describes famous people as surrounded by unusual events already at conception and birth, indicating God's special plan for a very important-person-to-be.

But were not your birth and mine also miracles from the moment we "cried" and the doctor said, "It's a boy/girl"? I am and will always be perhaps not a VIP but very precious in God's eyes. And I am and go on being only in God Who is continuously creating me. Awareness of this dependency keeps me humble and grateful as well (see Ps 22:11).

 OME! I will send you to Pharaoh, so that you may lead My people, the Israelites, out of Egypt. — Ex 3:10

MAR.
1

Fidelity to God's Call

In the call of any of the prophets, the Bible refers to our own call in life. And greatness is obedience to God's call with the serious effort to become what my Maker wants me to be.

The Bible never states that fidelity to our call is easy. That's why we are going to make it only if with all great men and women we see our call in life as related to God. Pray, "O Lord, do not stand far from me; O my help, make haste to aid me" (Ps 22:20), and He will answer as He did to Moses, "I will be with you" (Ex 3:12).

OD responded [to Moses], "I am Who am."

MAR.
2

The Triune God

Apparently this utterance is the source of the word "Yahweh," the personal name of God as the absolute and necessary Being.

Guided by the data of the Bible, we understand God as Father (related to creation), sending His Son or Word (for our salvation) and communicating the Spirit (related to our rebirth). You may pray with Paul, "Oh, the depth of the riches and wisdom and knowledge of God! ... From Him and through Him and unto Him are all things" (Rom 11:33, 36).

 HIS day shall be a memorial day for you, and you shall keep it as a memorial to the Lord. — Ex 12:14

MAR.
3

Memorial Celebrations

The author of Exodus refers to the Jewish Passover as something to celebrate. Celebration calls forth an experience of the past and makes this experience ours. Each celebration is a memorial—lest we forget God's loving care! Memorials of both our national and our Christian heroes are included.

Remembering keeps us grateful to fellow human beings and above all to God. Have you lately celebrated/remembered the birthday of your spouse, child, parent, or a dear friend? What about your regular celebration of the Eucharist? It too is a memorial!

I CARRIED you up on the wings of eagles and brought you here to Myself.

— Ex 19:4

God's Concern for Us

The Exodus event as celebrated annually is central in Jewish spirituality and in ours as well, since our paschal celebration, the passover from death to life, is fashioned after it.

The eagle carrying her young on her wings has inspired greatness, responsibility, and care throughout the centuries. Think, for example, of our baldheaded eagle! God carries you and me. Where in your own history did you experience that Divine concern?

MOUNT Sinai was totally wrapped in smoke, for the Lord descended upon it in fire. — Ex 19:18

Growth in Our Experience of God

Awareness of God present to you is of paramount importance for meditation as well as the peace and happiness that flow from it. Meditative prayer may sometimes result in a disclosure experience, in which you feel God's loving presence. Primitive people were aware of God's awesome greatness in the phenomena of nature. Medieval mystics experienced God as conditioned by their time and culture.

You may grow in awareness of God's loving care in your way the more you concentrate on Him in regular meditation. Pray, "Lead me in Your truth and teach me" (Ps 25:5).

YOU shall love the Lord, your God. . . .
Teach [these words] to your children.
Speak of them at home and abroad. . . .
—Deut 6:5-9

Symbolism of Love

Aware of the evil of legalism, the sacred author emphasizes the priority of love. In making ethical decisions, what is your guiding principle? Is it the law: What must I do? It should be love: What is the most loving thing to do in this particular situation?

The author insists on symbols and their meaningful use. What about our Christian symbols of love: wedding ring, valentine, crucifix on the wall, or golden cross on your neck chain?

Take heed not to forget the Lord . . .
when you have eaten and are full,
and have built splendid houses.
— Deut 8:11-14

Remember the Lord

American working ethics encourage lack of mindfulness. When you have made it financially, are successful in any field (marriage, children, school, health, job, even apostolate), bear in mind that you have not done it without God's help. You are not entitled to look down on fellow human beings who are less fortunate with or without any fault of their own.

Strive to remember the Lord and thank Him all your days. Pray, "You are my God, and I give You thanks" (Ps 118:28).

IRCUMCISE your hearts . . . and do not be stubborn any more.

— Deut 10:16

Love Rather Than Sacrifice

The Bible reminds us to keep rituals meaningful. Upon entering a church, you sprinkle yourself with holy water. This ritual should remind you of your Baptism, by which you are related to God in a covenant of love and entitled to partake in the Eucharistic celebration.

At such a celebration, you will pray, "We offer You in thanksgiving this holy and living sacrifice" (Eucharistic Prayer III). Hosea has God say, "For I desire love rather than sacrifice" (6:6). Stubborn people are usually not generous lovers! What about you?

 OU must love the foreigner, for you were once foreigners in the land of Egypt.

— Deut 10:19

Racism Is Un-Christian

We should heed these words carefully, especially now when there are so many legal and illegal aliens in our country. Their culture and behavior may be slightly different from ours, but we must accept them as they are. Racism is un-Christian and narrowminded.

Since speech betrays thinking, how is your language when mentioning different people in your church, school, commuter train, or on the job? Whenever negative self-talk is bothering you, do you try to switch to positive thinking?

INCE that time no prophet has arisen in Israel like Moses, whom the Lord knew face to face.

— Deut 34:10

MAR.
10

God's Spokespersons

No spokesperson of God has captured the imagination of both Jews and Christians as Moses has done. Jesus is even seen as a new Moses (Jn 1:21; 3:14; Acts 3:22; Heb 3:1-11), so close to God that final Biblical reflection calls Him God.

God speaks to us through fellow human beings. Learn from persons who are close to God—Moses, the Lord Jesus, and many more! Who are your favorite ones?

T that time the prophetess Deborah . . . was judging Israel. . . . The people of Israel came up to her for judgment. — Jdg 4:4-5

MAR.
11

Overcoming Male Chauvinism

Many a great leader has stated that to a large extent he owes his achievements to his wife, her wisdom, her inspiration, her dedication to a cause. Unfortunately, many men, clerics not excluded, are male chauvinists. They should strive to appreciate knowledge, wisdom, and sound judgment wherever God displays it. The Bible does this in Judges 4 and 5.

Right now in our Church there are conflicting opinions about the status of women, the majority of active members. Let us pray for God's guidance and bear with one another lovingly.

43

IDEON said, "If the Lord is with us, why then has all this [misery and disaster] befallen us?" —Jdg 6:13

Follow God's Plan

Gideon finally obeyed God's call to save Israel only because he believed God's assurance, "I will be with you" (Jdg 6:16). Bible and homilies in church teach that God is with us. But we too may ask, "Why has all this misery happened to me? If God is with me, can't He do better?"

The Lord told Gideon to send most of his soldiers home and defeat the Midianites with only three hundred men (Jdg 7:6). Perhaps you use too many "soldiers" of your own and don't let God do the job! Check and pray for light!

 HAVE been given a full account of what you have done for your mother-in-law. — Ru 2:11

Good Family Relationships

After the death of her husband, Ruth had left the land of her birth to take care of her mother-in-law Naomi. God granted her the honor of becoming an ancestor of the Messiah.

A senior member of the Bible study group, herself a mother-in-law several times, remarked, "I learn not only from Ruth but from Naomi. She must have been an extraordinary mother-in-law; otherwise Ruth would not have stayed with her." All of us should learn to keep family relationships alive lovingly and patiently.

AM a troubled woman. . . . I was only pouring out my soul to the Lord.

— 1 Sam 1:15

Prayer in Time of Unhappiness

Hannah's prayer to the Lord was heard. Despite previous sterility she bore a son.

Time and again, the Bible stresses the power of prayer, though God does not always answer our prayers the way we want. Whatever our reason for unhappiness we should follow Hannah's example. And we should be appreciative like Hannah who prayed, "My heart rejoices in the Lord, and my horn [symbol of strength] is exalted in my God" (1 Sam 2:1).

 PEAK, Lord, for Your servant is listening.

— 1 Sam 3:9

Prayerful Listening

Samuel did as he was told to do. When he went to sleep in his place, the Lord came and revealed His presence (1 Sam 3:10). Prayerfully listening may be more important than verbal prayer. Listening results in obedience to God's call and openmindedness to change priorities.

We must listen not only to Bible and sermon but to fellow human beings and happenings around us as well. A child's remark or the need of another human being may be God's call to you. Did you hear such a call recently and did you listen? Pray as Samuel did!

YOU have neither defrauded us, nor oppressed us, nor taken anything from anyone. —1 Sam 12:4

Honesty—Love for Others

It was the general opinion that Judge Samuel was an honest man. Honesty is a down-to-earth sign of real love for other human beings.

The Bible invites us to follow Samuel's example. We must never take advantage of anyone—in our business, our home, or our religious community. Perhaps not all friends and coworkers agree. Do we have the courage to be honest regardless of what others say and do? "The just man finds refuge through his honesty" (Prov 14:32).

DAVID overcame the Philistine with a sling and a stone . . . and did it without a sword in his hand.

— 1 Sam 17:50

Doing Our Part

In story form, the Bible teaches us to trust in God rather than in human ingenuity. This, trust, however, may not become a pretense for sloth and laziness. When I am sick, I go to my physician not a faith healer. Parents love their children intelligently, don't spoil them, dialogue with them, give good example, and only then prayerfully trust that God will be with them.

Check whether you keep a balance between doing your part and having faith in God. Pray for guidance!

NSTEAD [the rich man] took the poor man's lamb and made it into a meal for his visitor. — 2 Sam 12:4

MAR. 18

Sin and Repentance

Nathan's parable of which the present citation is part refers to King David's adultery. Since wives were paid-for possessions, adultery was mainly a sin against the seventh commandment: "You shall not steal." David already had many wives, yet he stole the "lamb," the wife, of Uriah.

A Church Father comments, "King David sinned as most kings do. He repented, however, as most kings don't do." Do I repent?

E [Joseph] rose, took the Child and His mother, and traveled to the land of Israel. —Mt 2:21

MAR. 19

Fidelity to Commitments

Joseph comes through as a man who accepts responsibility for a once made commitment. There were threats to his family (see Mt 2:13-18), but he does not dodge his responsibility. Sociologists mention a declining willingness in our culture to be faithful to commitments. Half of all marriages end up in divorce. Priests and religious have defected. Whom can we trust?

Check your own fidelity. And if you are a parent or educator, what values do you instill in your children? Pray for fidelity.

HEN the queen of Sheba beheld Solomon's great wisdom . . . she was overcome.

MAR. 20

— 1 Ki 10:4

Wisdom in Daily Life

"All Israel" had even a better understanding. "They perceived that the wisdom of God was in [the king]" (1 Ki 3:28).

Wisdom, insight, good judgment, efficient. management are well paid-for values in business. We need wisdom in daily life, in dealing with spouse and children, in a parish council meeting, and on the job. You get it by listening to intelligent people. You find it in your Bible. Pray, "Teach me wisdom" (Ps 119:66).

HE Lord said to [Elijah]: "Go to Zarephath of Sidon and dwell there. I have commanded a widow there to feed you."

MAR. 21

— 1 Ki 17:9

Experiencing God in Our Life Situation

The Bible tells us how bedouins and croppers experience God in their situation. A holy man of God is usually in the picture. There is drought in the land, hence famine. Elijah the prophet intervenes. The widow and her son survive, but faith in God is the condition.

The Bible teaches us about experiencing God in our life situation. Things did not go your way. Were you aware of God? Was perhaps a friend the "holy person" who appeared? Your Bible was on your book shelf! And what about your faith?

FTER the fire there was a still small voice.

—1 Ki 19:12

MAR. 22

Seeing God in the Ordinary

The somewhat clamorous prophet Elijah challenges the prophets of Baal to see if their god or Yahweh would really answer prayers. The God of Israel wins the contest, which calls forth the wrath of Queen Jezebel on Elijah. Hidden in a cave on Mount Carmel, he prays and experiences God passing by—not in a heavy wind nor in an earthquake nor in a fire but in a still small voice. A lesson for the fiery prophet!

Don't look for God in the spectacular! Find Him in the eyes of your spouse, a child, a friend. Any "thing of beauty," goodness, or concern is a sign of God's loving presence.

ABOTH answered him [King Ahab], "The Lord forbid that I should give you the inheritance of my ancestors."

— 1 Ki 21:3

MAR. 23

Working for Justice

The pattern of the narrative—King Ahab stealing a poor man's vineyard and killing him, the involvement of a woman, and a prophet announcing God's wrath—follows closely the story of David's adultery (2 Sam 11:12). The Bible condemns injustice.

Are you concerned about social justice; do you check your candidates' ideas about it when voting; and are you fair in doing business?

HEY bowed their heads and worshiped the Lord, with their faces to the ground. — Neh 8:6

MAR. 24

Worshiping with the Body

The scene is the restored Temple of Jerusalem after Ezra the scribe has read the Law. Once in Dakar, Senegal, I saw thousands of Muslim men kneeling in the streets, bowing down, their faces to the ground, praying.

Liturgical behavior is conditioned by culture. But are the gestures that we make (such as the sign of the cross, genuflection, bowing, kneeling, standing, and shaking hands) meaningful and do they enhance devotion? Soul and body should worship our Maker. This requires faith and overcoming our self-consciousness!

―――――――

HE Holy Spirit will come upon you, and the power of the Most High will overshadow you. — Lk 1:35

MAR. 25

Faith in the Face of a Mystery

Dealing with a mystery, Mary has doubts and questions: "How can this be, since I have no relations with a man?" (Lk 1:34). Yet, in faith, she accepts: "May it be done to me according to your word" (Lk 1:38).

Even Christians do not have ready-made answers for all questions. Facing them, you don't dodge them. Ask for information from more than one expert, read, and by all means pray for courage to surrender as Mary did. "Blessed is she who believed" (Lk 1:45).

APHAEL said . . . : "I did not come to you out of any favor on my part, but because it was God's will."

—Tob 12:18

Gratitude for God's Caring Love

In a folktale we learn about God's caring protection for all of us. Whether God shows His care through angels, humans, or events in life is of little importance.

Recently, where and how have you experienced God's love for you? Raphael said, "Therefore, continue to thank [God] daily" (Tob 12:18). With the psalmist pray, "I will thank You forever for what You have done" (Ps 52:11).

UDITH led all Israel in this song of thanksgiving . . . : "O Lord, You are great and glorious. . . ."

— Jdt 15:14; 16:13

Respect for Women

Judith, who was "beautiful in appearance" (Jdt 8:7), is called "the glory of Jerusalem, the great joy of Israel, the splendid boast of our nation" (Jdt 15:9) even though her great deed was quite bloody—cutting off Holofernes' head (Jdt 13:8).

The Liturgy sees Judith (because of her dedication and faith) as a paradigm of Mary, the Mother of Jesus. All males should foster a great appreciation and respect for women. God's greatness is embodied in them no less than in men! If a male reader, what about your talk about women? If a woman, thank God!

ING [Ahasuerus] said to Esther, "What is it you request? It shall be granted you." . . . Esther replied: "O king, . . . spare the lives of my people." — Est 7:2-3

MAR. 28

Using Our Talents for Others

In secular literature, female characters use their charms and ingenuity usually to achieve their own goals. In the Biblical narrative about Esther, the heroine uses her beauty and wisdom to serve her people at the risk of her life.

What are my talents and how do I use them to serve my family, my congregation, my coworkers, or my fellow students? Pray: God, help me to realize that all I am is Your gift, which I must use as an instrument of Your love.

HE Lord speaks: "Sons have I reared and brought up, but they have disowned Me!" — Isa 1:2

MAR. 29

Sharing Disappointment with God

As a celibate priest, I feel ashamed sometimes when parents share their worry about a teenager or even a grown-up child, who has gone astray: dope, alcohol, broken marriage, crime! I can share their anxiety only as an outsider. Isaiah sees God, our Father, as disappointed: "An ox knows its owner . . . but Israel [you and me?] has not known Me" (Isa 1:3).

As children of God we should not forsake Him. Whether we are parents or educators, we should not expect perfect success. Share your disappointments with the Lord!

ND daughter Zion is left like a booth in a vineyard, like a shed in a cucumber garden. —Isa 1:8

Darkness of Faith

Isaiah refers to temporary shelters ("booth," "shed") that used to be set up for those who watched over the harvest and were later abandoned. In moody moments we may feel rejected by a loved one, a friend, who should be more attentive, or even God in our prayer life. Where is God? It is the darkness of faith, which all who meditate experience every so often.

In Isaiah, it is daughter Zion's own fault, the result of her sinful behavior. When in this state, check your own conscience first. Possibly you have to repent for some fault!

————————

VEN though you recite many prayers, I will not listen. . . . Seek after justice, relieve the oppressed, hear the plea of the orphan, and defend the widow.

— Isa 1:15-17

Prayer and Works

Even daily Mass attendance and frequent prayers don't make sense if active Christian charity does not accompany them. Stating "I don't harm anybody" is not enough.

Ask yourself constantly, "What is the most loving thing to do in this situation?" It could be going to the nursing home to see a lonely old person instead of going to the evening Mass! "Learn to do good" (Isa 1:17) with God's help, of course.

OW has she, the faithful city, which was so upright, become an adulteress!
— Isa 1:21

APR.

1

Keeping Love Alive

For Israel, all sin is infidelity to perfect love. Married people know that love is a touchy thing. It is ruined more by what spouses fail to do than by positive harm. Apply this to all your relations, including the one with God, or "you shall become like an oak with withered leaves, like a garden that lacks water" (Isa 1:30).

Love that is moth-eaten does not last. Keep it fully alive! Never forget that love and faith should be dealt with in the same way. They are very much akin.

ROM Zion shall go forth the law, and the word of the Lord from Jerusalem.
— Isa 2:3

APR.

2

Listening to the Church

We Catholics insist on living our faith together and see the Church community as mediating in time and space the word and work of our risen Lord. That's why we follow instruction forthcoming from Zion-Jerusalem-Rome.

For example, the Church commits herself to a "preferential option for the poor." Could you write your elected officials to do something about ghetto situations in your hometown and about poverty abroad? We are co-responsible!

THE Lord of hosts has a day in store for all the proud and lofty.
— Isa 2:12

APR.

3

The Day of the Lord

"The Day of the Lord" is mentioned quite often in the Bible as a warning for those who could not care less about God. It is also a plea for patience. When we see injustice, abuse of human rights, and ruthless dictators having things their way, we may raise the question, "Why does a loving God not step in right now?"

The question becomes even more urgent when it concerns injustice done to us. Do we have patience and leave retribution to the Lord? We must pray for faith, for "the haughtiness of men will be brought low" (Isa 2:17).

WHAT more could have been done for My vineyard than I have done for it?
— Isa 5:4

APR.

4

Our Contributions

The Vineyard Song, one of the highlights of Hebrew literature, describes God's disappointment with the "House of Israel"—all of us, His chosen ones. "He looked for the crop of good grapes, but it yielded only wild grapes" (Isa 5:2).

What about your productivity as a Christian? What do you contribute to your family, parish, or religious community to make it a more beautiful and a happier family of believers? Each of us is responsible so that God can be pleased with His vineyard. What do you do?

OE to those who are wise in their own eyes, and prudent in their own sight! —Isa 5:21

APR. 5

Prudence Can Be Faulty

A young medical doctor who had lost his faith condescendingly told me, "We have that over with!" He still believed in an Ultimate Reality but found organized religion superfluous.

His prudence did not realize that there are very few things we do alone—especially in the field of faith, which must be treated like love. Both are tangibles! Togetherness is mandatory for both lovers and believers. What about your prudence, which is not the same as an M.A. or a Ph.D? Ask your Maker for real wisdom, and use the means to keep relationships alive.

SAW the Lord seated on a high and exalted throne. . . . Seraphim were stationed above Him. . . . And they cried out: "Holy, holy, holy is the Lord of hosts!" — Isa 6:1-3

APR. 6

A Humbling Experience

Isaiah had a vision, a disclosure experience. Once in a great while it is granted to those who meditate regularly. It is a valuable moment for which we should be grateful.

This experience made Isaiah humble: "Woe is me, I am ruined! For I am a man of unclean lips" (Isa 6:5). Who am I? A red blinker on a radio mast: on—out! Yet God knows and loves me. Think of this when you sing your "Holy, holy, holy" in church next Sunday!

HEN I heard the voice of the Lord saying, "Whom shall I send? Who will go for us?" And I cried out, "Here I am. Send me!"   —Isa 6:8

APR.

7

On Mission for the Lord

When we are unaware of our call and are not living up to it, life becomes meaningless and ultimately unsatisfying. Suicide is a number-one plague in this country among those who have plenty materially. Why?

I am "great" as long as I carry out my responsibilities and strive to be a loving person. How much did you give yourself recently? You don't want your epitaph to read: "Here lies N. He never bothered anybody!"

HE virgin [Hebrew, *almah:* young maiden] shall be with child and give birth to a Son, and they shall name Him Immanuel ["With us is God"].

—Isa 7:14

APR.

8

Immanuel—With Us Is God

Jerusalem was threatened by surrounding enemies. Through Isaiah, God promised him a sign of Divine protection; but rather than trusting his Maker, the king turned to Assyria.

Although Isaiah may not have known the full force latent in this oracle, Church tradition sees the promise of "With us is God" fully realized. in the Child born of Mary. When like Ahaz you are tempted to depend too much on your own ingenuity, especially in time of distress, and become depressed as a result, think of "With us is God" in the Lord Jesus.

THE people walking in darkness have seen a great light.

— Isa 9:2

The Light of the World

When my car broke down on a dark and lonesome country road and I had no flashlight, I felt helpless. Would that I had a light! Life can be that way—with or without our fault. Both having no flashlight in your car and having destroyed a precious relationship are human. We Christians have a light, however.

When down in the dumps, do I open my Bible, find a quiet place, concentrate and find the Lord Jesus, "light of the human race" (Jn 1:3)? He counsels us on how to restore relations.

WOE to those who make unjust laws . . . to deprive the poor of their rights and withhold justice from the oppressed. — Isa 10:1-2

Concern for Social Justice

This rich country of ours has thousands of people who are homeless, sleep in the streets, and eat in charity soup kitchens. The Churches step in, and we should support private charity. But what about both our domestic and our foreign policy on social justice?

Is your diocese involved, for example, in ensuring civil rights? What does your parish council do? What can you do? Are you acquainted with both the Pope's and the American Bishops' statements on social justice?

THE spirit of the lord will rest upon Him.

— Isa 11:2

APR.
11

Voting and Praying

Isaiah writes about an anointed king to come. He dreams about a perfect administration, like the one that candidates for office promise during their campaigns. "He will judge the poor with justice and decide in favor of the poor" (Isa 11:4). Hence preferential option for the poor and affirmative action?

Reading the American Bishops' Pastoral Letters on the economy and on war and peace may be helpful. Exercise your voting rights and pray for those in public office.

THEN the wolf shall dwell with the lamb, and a leopard shall lie down with the goat.

— Isa 11:6

APR.
12

Working for Peace

Here again we have a dream of a perfect society! The United Nations solving all disputes peacefully! "Never again!" is written on the Dunkirk monument on the World War I battlefield in Flanders. The surrounding trenches tell the story of what happened.

Peace on earth? What about starting in your family or religious community? Are you a peacemaker at work or school and in your parish? It requires positive thinking and being aware that the dream will be fully realized only in Messianic times!

59

GOD indeed is my savior, I will trust and remain unafraid.

— Isa 12:2

Turning to God Our Savior

What did God rescue you from? Perhaps from yourself? A person full of negative talk about self is his/her own enemy. A pessimist is an unhappy person. Indeed, we are responsible for how we feel and must consequently learn to control our thoughts and feelings.

Do we have reasons to be optimists even when things don't go our way? Turn to your Savior and His message in prayerful meditation. "God, deliver my soul from the sword. . . . Rescue me from the lion's mouth" (Ps 22:21-22).

SHOUT aloud and sing for joy, O city of Zion, for great in your midst is the Holy One of Israel!

—Isa 12:6

Singing at Liturgical Services

Singing should be part and parcel of our weekend worship services. A music-filled celebration enhances our awareness that the "Holy One" is in our midst. Choir rehearsals demand time and patience, but they are really Christian service! We should appreciate our church choir and be part of it if invited. Both choir and congregation must shout with joy.

If your congregation is still behind, turn to the parish council, every so often visit a church that has "soulful" singing, and listen to good religious music on TV or records.

LORD, . . . you have fulfilled Your wonderful plans of long ago.
— Isa 25:1

APR. 15

Gratitude for God's Blessings

Think of your past: persons who have shaped your life—parents, teachers, friends. Who would you be if such persons had not crossed your path? Events: that stay in the hospital, your graduation, meeting your spouse, your wedding, religious vows, ordination. . . . Do you see God's "wonderful plans" fulfilled in you?

Every Sunday, you hear the invitation "Let us give thanks to the Lord, our God." Always reflect a moment: "Where did God bless me last week, and did I show my gratitude?"

———————

OU have been a refuge for the poor, a refuge for the needy in distress, a shelter from the storm, and a shade from the heat. — Isa 25:4

APR. 16

Helping the Needy

Not being in the category of the needy, going through a relatively peaceful period of life, and sitting in an air-conditioned room, we may easily believe this statement of Isaiah.

"The Lord God will wipe away the tears from all faces" (Isa 25:8). He does it, however, through other human beings. And we should not leave it up to the charity sisters of Mother Teresa to do. What about saying a kind word to a coworker "in distress," offering transportation on Sunday morning to a less fortunate parishioner, or visiting an elderly shut-in?

B EHOLD, this is our God; to Him we looked to save us. — Isa 25:9

Look to the Lord!

Did we really look to the Lord "to save us" when we had to make that important decision, when our duties accumulated, or when the children disappointed us? Or must we confess, "Like a woman about to give birth, who writhes and cries out in her pains, so were we . . ., O Lord. We gave birth to wind [and] have not achieved salvation" (Isa 26:17-18).

In whatever we may be involved, but especially in volunteer church work, we may give birth to wind if our motivation is not rooted in the Lord and we don't look to Him to save us.

Y OUR perversity is . . . as though what is made should say of its maker, "He did not make me!" —Isa 29:16

Authentic Achievements

We have won the West, built skyscrapers and plants in the East, and are proud of our wheat, corn, and cotton fields in between. America the beautiful! Are we aware, however, of God's "Woe to the obstinate children, . . . who carry out plans that are not Mine"? (Isa 30:1).

Achievements at the expense of others are certainly not God's plans! Am I considerate? Or do I live by a double standard: one for Sundays and one for the other days of the week? Pray, "You are my Lord. Apart from You I have no good thing" (Ps 16:2).

THE meek will find fresh joy in the Lord, and the poor will exult in the Holy One of Israel. —Isa 29:19

The Danger of Success

It is said that religion did better when Catholics were still poor first generation immigrants. Probably, God's word of old is still true: "So Jacob [God's people] ate his fill. . . . He spurned the God Who made him" (Deut 32:15).

Whatever your success in life may be: family, business, health, work, be appreciative! Let it never be true that "you forgot the God Who fathered you" (Deut 32:18) and that "the meek" put you to shame. You may pray, "O Lord, . . . You have made my lot secure" (Ps 16:5).

BY waiting and by calm you shall be saved, in quiet and in trust shall be your strength. — Isa 30:15

Cultivating Christian Patience

Calm and patience are not always popular virtues. Not all human beings are as efficient and quick-acting as we think we are! Apply this when you are waiting in line for bus or train, stuck behind an incredibly slow driver in heavy traffic, or faced with a difficult spouse, parent, or child in family life.

And what about life in a religious community with elderly members endlessly repeating their stories of bygone days! "Trust" means trust in the Lord as well as in the basic goodness of other human beings.

E [God] will be gracious to you at the sound of your cry; as soon as He hears He will answer you. —Isa 30:19

APR. 21

Love Is the Basis

Some people maintain that the old catechisms of the Faith stressed fear of punishment more than love as basic to our relationship with our Creator. This may or may not be true.

What is true is that you must have a living relationship of mutual love with God and a consequent love of neighbor. Only then will Isaiah's statement be meaningful to you and you will "cry," "Restore to me the joy of Your salvation" (Ps 51:14).

AY to those who are fearful of heart: Be strong, fear not! Behold, your God will come with vindication. — Isa 35:4

APR. 22

Comforter of the Frightened

Stage: pastoral home visit with a family of nine at 9:00 P.M. The parents are worried. School was out at 3:00 P.M. Their fifteen-year-old son has not shown up yet. Where is he? What is he doing? Has something happened? As a priest, I am concerned, but the young man is not my son. I do not have to stay up and wait. . . . I feel somehow ashamed.

Hearts are often frightened. The one who really understands is our Maker. He will come to save, perhaps through you and me! We should be concerned and turn to God!

WHEN the eyes of the blind will be opened, and the ears of the deaf will be unstopped. — Isa 35:5-6

God's Word to Us Today

Does prayerful meditation on the Bible change us? The Bible is God's word to you and me today; in it He comes "with vindication" (Isa 35:4) to save you. Does daily contact with the Bible open our eyes, clear our ears, and give us stamina to "be doers of the word and not hearers only, deceiving ourselves" (Jas 1:22)?

When you are feeling "lame" and inefficient and in need of power to keep moving, pray to your Maker, "Look upon me, and have mercy on me; give strength to Your servant" (Ps 86:16).

 SPEAK tenderly to Jerusalem, and tell her that her service [servitude and exile] has been completed. — Isa 40:1-2

Paradigms of God's Loving Care

The exodus from Egypt and the return from captivity in Babylon are beloved paradigms, used by writers of both Testaments to describe God's loving care and salvation from all evil.

Isaiah describes the return of the exiles: "The glory of the Lord will be revealed and all mankind will see it together" (Isa 40:5). Matthew sees this vision fulfilled in the freedom and salvation brought about in the kingdom of God as established by Jesus here on earth and to be fully realized in the hereafter (Mt 3:3) We should be grateful for being part of it.

GOD will feed His flock like a shepherd; He will gather the lambs in His arms and gently lead the ewes.

— Isa 40:11

APR.
25

Relying on God in Time of Trouble

Life can be rough, as it was for the Jews rebuilding their homeland after the exile in Babylon! It may be our own fault: "I rushed into marriage"; "I didn't finish my education"; "I didn't think!" Often the darkness that surrounds us is not our fault: ennui over prayer; dull worship services; family or job problems.

What can we do? How do we integrate our faith into a process of healing? Read Isaiah's words again! You could pray, "[God,] keep me as the apple of Your eye" (Ps 17:8).

WITH whom can you compare God? To what image can you liken Him? —Isa 40:18

APR.
26

God the Ineffable!

Since we don't know an adequate definition of God, the Bible usually describes Him as related to us and (because of its man-oriented culture) as male: king, judge, army commander, father, a few times as mother, shepherd, gardener, spouse, friend, creator, maker, potter, Lord, and ultimately as Love.

God is so great! In our dim human condition, we can only grope for comparisons and add mentally, "Much greater than. . . ." How do you experience God? How do you react?

HOUGH EVEN young men grow tired and weary, . . . those who hope in the Lord will renew their strength. They will soar on eagle's wings.

— Isa 40:30-31

APR. 27

Renewed in God

The deterioration of the human system starts at an early age. Athletes are most aware of it. But getting up in age, all of us experience failing stamina. Sometimes it is boredom that causes lack of initiative. It could be wearying love!

With God it is different. "He does not grow tired or weary. . . . He gives strength to the weary and makes the vigor of the weak abound" (Isa 40:28-29). When you are weary, pray, "Come, Holy Spirit, fill the hearts of Your faithful and kindle in them the fire of Your love" (Pentecost Liturgy). He may make you "soar" again!

AM the Lord, your God, Who hold your right hand and say to you, "Fear not; I will help you."

— Isa 41:13

APR. 28

Tapping All Resources!

Victor Frankle, a Jewish psychiatrist in Vienna, Austria, incorporates the client's religion in the healing process (called "logotherapy"). It is a good philosophy of life to tap both natural and religious resources to keep moving.

Check your resources. When down in the dumps with or without fault of your own, where do you turn? God is present to you both indirectly, in a physician, good friend, or counselor, and directly, in your prayer. "[Lord], deliver me according to Your word" (Ps 119:170).

EHOLD My Servant . . . upon Whom I have put My Spirit; He will bring forth justice to the nations. — Isa 42:1-2

APR.
29

The Servant of the Lord

This Servant may be an ideal Israel. Christian tradition sees this vision fulfilled in Jesus Christ. As the extension of the Lord Jesus and called to be an "ideal Israel," all of us are envisioned as such.

God's Spirit has been given to you and me. It is our task to bring forth justice and happiness to all around us not by making noise and a name for ourselves, but quietly. What about your charity and church work? your dedication in the family?

OU see many things but pay no attention; your ears are open, but you hear nothing. — Isa 42:20

APR.
30

The Value of Being Open

I recently met a mother of ten who will graduate from college soon. She needs the education and an adequate job. She said, "My eyes were opened too late!" Has a failure to see or listen hurt you in the past? Can you still restore the damage done? Indeed, do you develop the skill of seeing and listening? "Knowing everything in advance" backfires quite often.

What about your Bible? "I will lead the blind on their way; along paths unknown I will guide them" (Isa 42:16). Pray, "Teach me Your way, O Lord, and lead me on a level path" (Ps 27:11).

YOU are precious in My sight and honored, and . . . I love you.

— Isa 43:4

MAY 1

God's Undying Love for Us

Because God loves His people, He promises redemption and restoration. It is great that God loves us as we are, often in dire need of restoration: "Everyone who is called as [His] . . . whom [He] formed and made" (Isa 43:7). A widow once told me that her son had been mean to her, messed up his life with dope, deserted wife and child, and gone off to a big city. Then she said, "But I am his mother and I still love him!"

I am precious in God's eyes! "It is I, I, Who blot out . . . your offenses" (Isa 43:25). We do have reasons to be grateful!

BUT you do not call upon Me, O Jacob, for you have grown weary of Me, O Israel.

— Isa 43:22

MAY 2

God—the Tremendous Lover

Faith should be dealt with like love. Both are very sensitive values. Alienation is a constant possibility in each case. If you are weary of God (prayer, church, religion as such), how come? It didn't happen overnight. Spouses may blame one another, but you cannot blame God for getting weary—only yourself.

"I love You, O Lord, my strength" (Ps 18:2). In the marital situation, both spouses need to express their love every so often. Similarly, our love for God also needs to be expressed.

69

THUS says the Lord . . . Who formed you in the womb: Do not be afraid, O Jacob, My servant, the darling whom I have chosen.　—Isa 44:2

MAY 3

God Female?

The term of endearment "darling" indicates the intimate relationship of God to His people. The Bible is accused of describing God too exclusively as male and only seldom as female or mother. (There is no gender in God.)

But the authors of the Bible were more aware of God as female (mother and bride) than a superficial reading may suggest. "Darling" fits more in the mouth of a mother than a father, especially when God's creative activity is brought out as "formed you in the womb"!

ET the earth open wide and salvation bud forth; let justice also grow with it.　— Isa 45:8

MAY 4

Salvation as a Lifelong Process

The prophet sees salvation and justice to be realized as a growing process. This relates to children. As a parent, do you pray with your children and read a youth Bible? Some churches distribute children's bulletins. Do you do the suggested activities with them? What about your church school? Are you involved?

Do you see your own growth as a lifelong process? As in the marital relationship, it is either increasing or withering away! Can you honestly pray, "God, I love You"?

OE to him who quarrels with his Maker; a potsherd among the potsherds of the earth!

— Isa 45:9

MAY 5

Listening

When the will of God is clear, I should pray with Jesus, "Your will be done!" (Mt 26:42).

Most of the time, however, God's will is mediated to me through other human beings. When dealing with Bible and Church statements, I obey. But God may speak elsewhere also. Asked little Mary: "Papa, why do you talk so mean to my mammy?" "Wisdom . . . loosened the tongue of infants!" (Wis 10:21). Do you listen?

 VEN to your old age I am He, and even when your hair is gray I will bear you.

— Isa 46:4

MAY 6

Borne Up by God

A well known story: Faithfully, I was walking along the beach with the Lord. Two sets of footprints were left behind—one belonging to me and the other to the Lord. Looking back, I noticed that sometimes there was only one set—during the lowest time of my life. "How come, Lord? Why did You desert Me?" His answer: "During your time of suffering there was one set because it was then that I carried you."

Whether I am getting up in years or not, I should grow in awareness of God "bearing me" and be grateful!

EARKEN to Me, you fainthearted, you who are far from righteousness.

— Isa 46:12

Salvation Demands Willpower

Waiting for hours in the hot sun for an open air Mass with the Pope made many people faint. When a downpour came, hundreds who did not bring umbrellas left.

Patience, perseverance, and determination require willpower and finding what you are waiting for worthwhile. Isaiah has the Lord say, "My salvation will not tarry" (46:13). Pray for faith, willpower, and patience when you are fainthearted and the weather conditions of your life are less than favorable.

 OUR wisdom and your knowledge led you astray, and you said in your heart, "I am, and there is no one besides me"

— Isa 47:10

The Gift of Faith

One of my former students who was doing postgraduate work told me that he was through with the Church, priests, and bishops. He could do without God as well. After all, what do we know about the hereafter? John will find out if he is really self-sufficient when the first headwinds start buffeting him.

Like love, faith is a gift, which will not automatically be given again once you have thrown it out the window! "You have forsaken the fountain of wisdom!" (Bar 3:12). Your "wisdom" must come from somewhere. Be grateful for it!

T HE Lord called me from before my birth; from my mother's womb He has made mention of my name.

—Isa 49:1

God's Calling

Working with Chinese people in the Far East, I found out that names were not given to babies right away. Grandparents had to be consulted, names of ancestors had to be checked, and only then was a meaningful name given. Name-giving and calling for a task in life are one and the same in Biblical culture.

To us, God said, "You are My servant, . . . in whom I will show My splendor" (Isa 49:3). Reflect on your call in life and pray for strength.

AN a mother forget her infant, so as not to have pity on the child of her womb? And if she should forget, I will never forget you. — Isa 49:15

Maternal Aspects?

Whenever male chauvinism tempts me, I think of my own mother, her wisdom, patience, determination when necessary, dedication and tenderness, especially when one of the ten she bore was sick. How was she able to be that way, reflecting God's love to all ten of us? She was a prayerful and devout Christian!

Should we not be more aware of the maternal aspects of God and from that awareness draw assurance that we will not be forgotten? There is no gender in God!

EHOLD, the Lord God is my helper; who will condemn me? They will all wear out like a garment, and the moths will eat them up.   — Isa 50:9

Interdependence—A Sign of God's Presence

Whether we are suffering or not, we depend on one another. Spouses rely on each other. Children depend on their parents. Employers and employees are interdependent. We all need friends and those in the healing professions.

In this situation of interdependency, Christians see the presence of the Lord, Who continues His work of creation. Are we aware of this or do we turn for help that is not dependable? Chemical dependency eats one up like a moth!

OW beautiful upon the mountains are the feet of those who bring glad tidings.   — Isa 52:7

Gratitude for Faith

Meditating on this text, Paul asks, "How can they hear without a preacher?" (Rom 10:14). "Faith then depends on hearing, and hearing depends on the word of Christ" (Rom 10:17). Not all human beings are as favored as we are in having the Faith. But we do not have to worry about their salvation.

God takes care of all people of goodwill. But their journey goes through a much darker valley of fear, uncertainty, and superstition than ours. Let us be grateful for the Christian joy that is ours and announce it by word and example!

ET He bore our infirmities and carried our sorrows. . . . And by His bruises we are healed. —Isa 53:4-5

The Mystery of Vicarious Suffering

Both the "mystery of iniquity" (all human pain, Christ's included) and the "mystery of God's mercy" can only be approached, not fully explained. Isaiah deals with the mystery of God's Servant suffering for others.

Were the deaths of the civil rights workers in the sixties necessary to heal a racist society and as such "salvific"? Christian tradition sees Isaiah's vision fulfilled in the suffering Jesus. As sinners, let us be grateful for being healed.

———————

OD sent His Son, born of a woman. —Gal 4:5

Jesus Our Savior!

In meditating on "salvation," our starting point must be God's loving initiative. He sends His wisdom, word, light, analogously "Son," made tangible in Jesus of Nazareth. And in Him, His image (Col 1:15), Almighty God shows what a meaningful and consequently happy life is all about. Jesus is the exemplary cause of my salvation, and He also saves me by His constant prayer up till now (see Heb 7:25).

Do I accept the Lord Jesus, God's image, as directive in my life and constantly interceding for me at God's right hand? If so, He is my "personal savior! " Thank God for sending Him!

H E [Jesus] was delivered up for our sins and was raised for our justification.

MAY **15**

— Rom 4:25

Biblical Figures of Speech

The authors of the New Testament use metaphors (figures of speech) like sacrifice, reconciliation, expiation, redemption, and justification to approach the mystery of Jesus' involvement in our restored relationship with God. These may lead us to see Christ going to His death as a vicarious Victim Who pays our debt to the Father, hence God as a sadist Who claims the death of Jesus.

To avoid this error, we must see them as figures of speech that tell us about God's love and Christ's concern for us!

G OD so loved the world that He gave His only-begotten Son, so that everyone who believes in Him might not perish but might have everlasting life.

MAY **16**

—Jn 3:16

In the Cross Is Our Salvation!

God made His wisdom, word, light, as forthcoming from Him "His Son," visible in Jesus. When bitten by serpents, the Israelites were restored to health by looking at the bronze serpent that Moses had lifted up (Num 21:9).

So we must look at God's incarnated wisdom, Jesus, lifted up on the cross in order to be healed and saved (see verse 14). Do I ever look at the crucifix in my church, on the wall in my home? "So I will cherish the old rugged cross!"

THE Father of glory . . . worked in Christ and raised Him from the dead. — Eph 1:17, 20

MAY 17

The Paschal Mystery

The Bible does not adequately explain human suffering or the passion and cruel death of Jesus. We may not attribute to God what human injustice has done to our Lord. God transcends the negative aspects of our history not by just permitting them but by overcoming them, namely in the resurrection.

Meditating on the paschal mystery is salvific, since we see it as emanating from unconditional fidelity to a call that was valuable for God and inspirational for suffering humankind.

JESUS . . . suffered outside the gate to sanctify the people through His own blood — Heb 13:12

MAY 18

Saved through Christ's Self-Offering

The author of Hebrews experiences salvation from God in the Lord Jesus. He expresses this in the terminology of his religious culture. He describes Jesus as a Jewish High Priest offering a bloody sacrifice to make up for sins.

By keeping in mind that he is using figurative language, we eliminate all sadistic and even cannibalistic connotations, as if God, to be placated, wanted the cruel death of His Son and the literal drinking of His blood. Thank God for your salvation, which comes from Him in and through Jesus' giving of self.

B Y a single offering He has made perfect for all time those who are being sancti- fied. —Heb 10:14

Dedication to Our Calling in Life

The meaning of Jesus' life is found in His death on the cross, seen as a free gift of self, closely related, though, to His controversial ministry that had to result in it. Jesus did not want His death (Mt 26:39), but He accepted it by persevering in the work He had to do.

Meditate on Jesus' suffering as emanating from dedication to His calling in life! As Christians, we are consecrated to the Lord. Let us be grateful and persevere doing our task in life even when the consequences may be risky.

———————

I F you take it patiently when you suffer for doing what is good, this is a grace before God. It is for this that you have been called, because Christ also suffered for you.

— 1 Pet 2:20-21

Suffering for Others

If mysteriously it is God's will that you suffer, it is better to suffer for doing good than for doing evil (see 1 Pet 3:17). The author is thinking of suffering from which God can draw good for others—that "they [the Gentiles] may see your good works and glorify God in the day of visitation" (1 Pet 2:12).

Are you willing to see your pain and frustration as suffering "for others"? Like Christ, you are called to do so by being an example and praying for them.

VEN if you should suffer . . . always be prepared to give an answer to anyone who asks you for a reason for the hope that is in you. — 1 Pet 3:14-15

MAY 21

Be a Challenge to Others

Those who suffer will "put to shame" (1 Pet 3:16) their defamers—they will lead them to instant reflection and ultimate conversion! Christ did this for us. He "also suffered for sins once for all, the just for the unjust, that He might lead us to God" (1 Pet 3:18).

"Therefore, since Christ suffered in the flesh, arm yourself with the same intent" (1 Pet 4:1). When suffering, be a challenge to others—but with gentleness and reverence! (see 1 Pet 3:16).

 E [Jesus] had to become like His brothers in all things, so that He might become a merciful and faithful high priest before God to expiate the sins of the people. —Heb 2:17

MAY 22

Reconciliation and Consecration

The tape on which all our evil deeds were registered is erased so that nobody, not even God, can listen anymore. To forgive but not forget is human. God does both. "I will no longer remember their sins and their evildoing" (Heb 10:17). And reconciliation does not mean only cleansing but also consecrating-dedicating us to God (see Heb 10:10).

Are you aware of and living up to your Christian dignity? Dedication has something to do with love!

HE will bear a Son and you are to name Him Jesus, for He will save His people from their sins. —Mt 1:21

MAY 23

Salvation Only in Jesus

In contrast to our culture, in Biblical setting the name assigned to a baby was considered an essential constituent of its bearer. "Jesus" means "God saves." History knows many "saviors": great kings, freedom fighters, civil rights workers! Peter denies that salvation comes through anyone other than Jesus: "There is salvation in no one else, for there is no other name . . . by which we are to be saved" (Act 4:12).

We share this awareness in faith. When you don't see a way out, turn to Jesus!

 HE Gentiles shall hope in Him. —Rom 15:12

MAY 24

A Living Sign of Hope

Are we still able to make our hope credible to people of our time and culture? It concerns our restored relationship with God, which does away with alienation and which is ours through Jesus. He is still alive although He lived 2000 years ago and God's love and wisdom was made tangible in Him as never before in any human being. This hope depends on God's gift of faith and the example of Christians!

Pray, "God, make me a living sign of hope for those who are groping for the peace and happiness that I find in Jesus."

RAISE a glad cry, O barren one, who did not bear. . . . Your descendants . . . shall inhabit the desolate cities. — Isa 54:1, 3

MAY 25

Appreciation for the Church

Depicted as a wife barren and deserted, Jerusalem now finds herself with innumerable children, the exiles returning from Babylon. Paul applies this text to the Church, the new Jerusalem, who is our mother (Gal 4:26). We are "children of the promise" (Gal 4:28).

Are we appreciative for having a church home? And are we sharing? Your congregation may have "lost sheep." Your effort, prayer, and example could perhaps populate your church with them!

FOR a brief moment I forsook you, but with great compassion I will take you back. — Isa 54:7

MAY 26

Apologizing to God and Others

Isaiah is aware of our intimate relationship with God: "For your Maker is your husband" (Isa 54:5). Hence any sin is seen as infidelity. Perhaps you have lost your first favor and are "like a wife married in youth and then cast off." However, "the Lord calls you back," and with enduring love He takes "compassion on you" (Isa 54:6-8).

What about your relationships? Do you keep them alive? Do you have trouble apologizing when you have failed both as related to other human beings and as related to your Maker?

81

Y love shall never depart from you nor shall My covenant of peace be shaken, says the Lord. — Isa 54:`0

Security in God

Meditating on our bridal relationship with God, Isaiah emphasizes security. It is what especially the bride is expecting. As related to God, we are the more vulnerable party. Perhaps you are "afflicted, storm-tossed, and unconsoled" (Isa 54:11). You worry about your teenagers. But God assures you, "Great shall be the peace of your children" (Isa 54:13).

Whatever your call in life, while doing your part, have faith in your Maker, Who is your husband (Isa 54:5).

EEK the Lord while He may be found, and call out to Him while He is near.
— Isa 55:6

Searching for God

God is near. "All you who thirst, come to the water!" (Isa 55:1). Are you thirsty for what the Lord has to offer you? Perhaps you "spend your money for that which is not bread [and] your labor for that which fails to satisfy" (Isa 55:2). Seek the Lord now! "Incline your ear and come to Me; listen, that you may have life," i.e., a meaningful life that satisfies you (Isa 55:3).

Isaiah stresses, "Seek - call - listen!" Do you? What about your Bible, the Sunday homily? What kind of friends do you have? God often speaks through a good friend!

Y thoughts are not your thoughts, neither are your ways My ways, says the Lord. — Isa 55:8

True Wisdom

Wherever we come across wisdom, good sense, and insight, we must see it as emanating from its source. But human thoughts, ours included, may be clouded by the human condition. True wisdom must be searched for patiently and often painfully. We check it against God's word: *the Bible and the guidance of the Church* (Isa 55:11). God's word shall achieve the end for which He sent it! (Isa 55:10-11).

What about your efforts? "How great are Your works, O Lord! How profound Your thoughts!" (Ps 92:6).

Y house shall be called a house of prayer for all peoples.

—Isa 56:7

Fellowship for All

Are "foreigners who join themselves to the Lord"—that is, minorities—welcome in your church? God says, "Their . . . sacrifices will be accepted on my altar" (Isa 56:6, 7). At Mass we pray, "We offer You in thanksgiving this holy and living sacrifice" (Eucharistic Prayer III). What can you do to make your parish a true family of believers?

Make your "handshake of peace" real. Is there anyone in church whose hand you would not shake? If so, don't be in the Communion line!

HE fasting that I choose [is]: . . . sharing your bread with the hungry, sheltering the homeless poor, and clothing the naked. — Isa 58:6-7

MAY 31

True Fasting

As Catholics who claim to follow Christ should we leave God's express wish about fasting up to the Salvation Army? That's what it looks like when we keep ourselves isolated in our comfortable suburban churches and parish centers and shun the inner city.

When have you visited a poor, old, and lonely person? What does your parish do for God's poor and deprived? Speak up when your parish council should change a few priorities!

———

F you turn back your foot on the sabbath from pursuing your own business . . . I will feed you with the heritage of Jacob, your father. — Isa 58:13-14

JUNE 1

Keeping Holy the Lord's Day

Worshiping your Maker regularly is Divine Law. Setting apart a special day to do it together reflects your Church's wisdom. There are very few things you keep on doing in the long run if your practice is not fed by the constant inspiration of co-believers in the same cause.

On Sundays, do you have a meal with the family participating? Do you refrain from "pursuing your own business" by doing your shopping, etc. on one of the other six days of the week?

EHOLD, the hand of the Lord is not too short to save, nor is His ear too dull to hear. — Isa 59:1

God Is Always Ready To Help

We trust in the Lord. He will listen and is able to help. But what if we don't do our part of the job and "weave spider's webs . . . [which] are useless for clothing" (Isa 59:5-6)?

Do I spend enough time with my spouse? Do I spoil my children? If a teacher or a priest, do I diligently prepare my lessons or sermons? If a student, do I study hard? Do I impair my health by smoking, drinking too much, or overeating? If we are willfully deficient, we should not expect God to come to the rescue. Do your part and then turn to the Lord!

 IKE blind men we grope along the wall, feeling our way like people without eyes. — Isa 59:10

Taught by the Lord

Initially ignorant, every child has to go through a whole process of learning. And even mature people are groping for insight. How many philosophies of life are competing with one another! "Darkness covers the earth and thick darkness is over the peoples" (Isa 60:2).

Concerning the ultimate questions of life, however, we Christians are favored: "Upon you the Lord rises. . . . Nations shall walk by your light" (Isa 60:2-3). Pray, "I will . . . give thanks to Your name" (Ps 138:2).

E has sent Me to bring glad tidings to the afflicted, to bind up the brokenhearted. —Isa 61:1

Recognizing God's Healing

Isaiah said this in regard to the restoration of Jerusalem after the Babylonian exile. Luke has Jesus apply the saying to His mission (see Lk 4:18-20). However, the Nazarenes were not very eager to accept "glad tidings" and healing as coming from God through a local fellow. "Isn't this the son of Joseph?" (Lk 4:22). Who does He think He is?

It requires faith to accept healing when it comes through a dull sermon, a remark of a child, or the observation of the lady next door! Pray: "Lord, help me grow in my awareness of Your healing presence."

S the bridegroom rejoices over his bride so shall your God rejoice over you. — Isa 62:5

A Religion of Joy

As an altar boy, I heard preachers scaring God's sinful people. Happily, things have changed since Vatican II. Religion should be a joyful thing. God loves me: "You shall be called 'My Delight,'" (Isa 62:4). Therefore, "I rejoice greatly in the Lord" (Isa 61:10).

Meditate on your intimate relationship with God, Who is your spouse and pray: "How beautiful is Your love . . . how much better is Your love than wine" (SS 4:10).

THE kindnesses of the Lord I will recount, the glorious deeds of the Lord, because of all He has done for us. — Isa 63:7

JUNE 6

The Kindness of the Lord

The two hundreth anniversary of our Constitution was celebrated all over the country. Historical consciousness enhances the awareness of how we came to be whatever we are, and seen in the perspective of Faith it leads to gratitude. The Bible encourages recalling the favors ("kindnesses")of the Lord, mentioning the Exodus and the return from exile.

Think of one favor in your life for which you should be grateful. And voice your gratitude!

ALL our good deeds are like filthy rags; we have all shriveled up like leaves. — Isa 64:5

JUNE 7

Plea for Forgiveness

In the recent past, preachers may have overemphasized our sinfulness, resulting in long lines in front of the confessionals. Now the pendulum seems to have swung to another extreme. "Love—sweet love" sounds wonderful; but if our relationship to God is one of intimate love, it is the very reason why we so easily become like shriveled up leaves and sin by omission and indifference.

Apply this to your human relationships as well as to the direct relationship with your Maker. "Do not be so very angry, Lord, . . . for we are all Your people" (Isa 64:8).

87

S a mother comforts her child, so will I comfort you; you will find your comfort in Jerusalem.

—Isa 66:13

JUNE
8

God's Message of Comfort

During the Pope's visit to San Francisco in 1987, a woman told him in her speech, "I expect to be treated as a mature, educated, and responsible adult." Enjoying God's comfort and "fondled in [the] lap" of Mother Church (Isa 66:11-12) sounds good as time- and culture-bound poetry but may be conducive to authoritarianism.

Yet it is through Jesus, the Church, the Bible, and tradition that God mediates His message of comfort with or without a mother image of the Church. Anyway, we gratefully enjoy it "in the midst of the assembly" (Sir 15:5).

H, Lord God!" I said, "I do not know how to speak, I am only a child."

— Jer 1:6

JUNE
9

Courage in Adversity

Jeremiah tries to dodge his call as a prophet, i.e., spokesperson of Almighty God. He knows that advocating the good by word and example might result in isolation and even violent opposition. But the Lord tells him, "Do not be afraid before them, because I am with you" (Jer 1:8).

Do you fear isolation when you don't join certain malicious conversations and dubious actions on the job or in school? Remember, "The Lord watches over you. He is beside you at your right hand" (Ps 121:5). Pray for courage!

OES a virgin forget her jewelry, a bride her wedding ornaments? Yet My people have forgotten Me days without number. — Jer 2:32

JUNE 10

Persevering Love

Perseverance is required to be faithful to a commitment. God expects our covenant of love to last. He is faithful. Yet "My people have forgotten Me" (Jer 2:32).

Forgetfulness is the first sign of love on its way out! Love requires perseverance. Do you find it a value that enriches your life, hence worthwhile to work on? "Doing without" results in misery, loneliness, and depression. What do you do about "love" as related both to humans and to God? "Lord, teach me how to love!"

 UT not your trust in deceptive words and say, "This is the temple of the Lord! The temple of the Lord!" — Jer 7:4

JUNE 11

Putting Our Priorities in Order

Being proud of the church that you support is all right. But the building is no more than a symbol of God's presence and a necessary means for gathering. What are the priorities of your parish community? An ever more impressive parking lot or spending surplus money on a charity project, e.g., helping a parochial school to survive in a poor part of town?

If your congregation needs a status symbol, let it be your mutual love! Speak up, if necessary, and start "reform" with yourself!

S it I Whom they are harming? says the Lord. Are they rather not harming themselves, to their own shame? — Jer 7:19

12

We Are the Losers!

Scene: An unwed mother with five little children; gas to be cut off the next day. It is cold! I promise to pay the bill. "Thank you so much, Reverend," says she. "Sunday I'll come to your church." My reply: "No, you better go to your own [Baptist] church and thank God there!"

Who is doing a favor for whom when we go to church? When we drift away from God and neglect our prayer life, we hurt ourselves and may wind up "shamed!" We are the losers!

 VEN the stork in the air knows its seasons; turtledove, swallow, and thrush observe the time of their coming, but My people do not know the requirements of the Lord. — Jer 8:7

JUNE

13

Knowledge of God's Word

Every year a picture of the stork was in my hometown newspaper the day he was back. Is it our doom or pride that besides instinct we are blessed with intellect? "How can you say, 'We are wise'? . . . Since [the wise] have rejected the word of the Lord, what kind of wisdom do they have?" (Jer 8:8-9).

What about your acquaintance with the word of the Lord? Are there Bible study-prayer groups in your parish? What about your prayerful reflection on God's word?

S there no balm in Gilead? Is there no physician there? Why then is there no healing for the wound of the daughter of My people?
— Jer 8:22

Healing the Wounds of Sin

As a missionary, I have seen, smelled, and taken care of old, festering, and fly-infested wounds. Wounds are the paradigm of the "sin sick soul." The prophet laments, "I am disconsolate, and horror grips me" (Jer 8:21).

We Christians are fortunate to be aware that there is a "balm in Gilead" to heal the sin sick soul. See your Doctor, Who is also your Maker! Face to face confession as well as counsel in all fields is available. See your pastor. And make your act of contrition before Mass meaningful!

ET not the wise man glory in his wisdom, or the mighty man glory in his strength, or the rich man glory in his riches.
— Jer 9:22

JUNE
15

Glory in the Lord

A man remarked about a common acquaintance, "I beat him with my bank account!" We have made great progress in technology and genetics. Yet science will never be able fully to explain the mystery of life, love, happiness, frustration, pain, and finally death.

The prophet continues, "Let him who glories glory in this: that he understands and knows Me [God]" (Jer 9:23). Do I see all my achievements in their right perspective?

LL these nations are uncircumcised, **JUNE**
and even the whole house of Israel,
is uncircumcised in heart. —Jer 9:25 **16**

Living Up to Our Call

The prophet has the Lord say, "I will demand an account of all those who are circumcised only in their flesh" (Jer 9:24). Likewise, God will ask an account of all who have been initiated into the mystery of Christ by Baptism, the Eucharist, and Confirmation.

Am I, perhaps, uncircumcised in heart? Am I living up to my call of being a baptized Christian? Honesty and love are mandatory. Pretending to be what I am not classifies me as "unbaptized in heart." "Lord, help me to be honest and realistic with myself and with others."

 AN'S course is not within his own **JUNE**
choice, nor is it up to man to direct
his own step. —Jer 10:23 **17**

Accepting Our Fate

Referring to Peter's future crucifixion, Jesus said to him, "When you are old . . . someone else will gird you and lead you where you do not want to go" (Jn 21:18).

Taking my daily walk in the mall of our town, I see persons in wheelchairs. Why them and not me? I am grateful to my Maker and pray for strength to accept my fate when my turn comes. Whether young or old, our course may not be within our choice. We must do what Jesus said to Peter: "Follow Me" (Jn 21:19).

[THE Lord] made the whole house of Israel . . . My people, My renown, My praise, My glory. But they have not listened.

JUNE 18

—Jer 13:11

Behaving as God's People

We might hear the parents of teenagers saying these words. Can God be proud of you: His renown, His praise, His glory? Parents are frustrated when children listen more to their peers in school than to them.

Do I listen more to the TV commercials than to God's word, which challenges me to be His praise, His glory? The closeness of a love relationship requires careful attention to the wishes and feelings of the beloved, i.e., God!

———————

 LESSED is the man who trusts in the Lord. . . . He is like a tree planted by the water that sends out its roots by the stream.

JUNE 19

— Jer 17:7-8

Confidence in God

Jeremiah describes the happy state of those who trust in the Lord. They are like trees that have access to water and fear not the heat, for their "leaves remain green" (Jer 17:7-8).

When you go through a period of fatigue and dryness in prayer life, check first to see to what extent the dryness may be your own fault. Then send out your roots "by the stream" (Jer 17:8). Patiently keep contact with the source of inspiration, God, in Whom you "live and move and have [your] being" (Act 17:28).

SAY to myself, . . . I will not speak in [the Lord's] name anymore. —Jer 20:9

Getting through a Crisis of Faith

Jeremiah goes through a crisis of faith. At times, each one of us also does so. Does it make sense to remain faithful to my call in life as a dedicated spouse, parent, religious, or priest? Am I about to be a "burned out case," ready for early retirement? The prophet finds courage to persevere in "the Lord," Who "is with me, like a mighty warrior" (Jer 20:10-11).

Crises of faith and discouragements are part of the human condition. Try to handle them as Jeremiah did. Pray, "Answer me quickly, O Lord, for my spirit fails" (Ps 143:7).

 HY did I come forth from the womb, to see trouble and sorrow and to end my days in shame? — Jer 20:18

Respect for Life

In his crisis of faith, Jeremiah is desperate. He regrets that God did not dispatch him in the womb. However, though Jeremiah curses the day on which he was born, he entrusts himself to the Lord (Jer 20:14, 12).

When depressed I turn to the Lord. After all, with God in the picture, life is wonderful and worth living. Respect for life means cultivating it in all its aspects.

S king He will reign and govern wisely; He will do what is just and right in the land. —Jer 23:5

JUNE 22

Working for God's Kingdom

During political disaster, people yearn for a better future, giving rise to revolts seen daily on TV. The New Testament writers saw the above oracle fulfilled in the "Kingdom of God" as inaugurated by a Messianic king, the Lord Jesus.

As Christians who are the extension of Jesus Christ, it is our task to work on the anticipation of God's kingdom on this side of the grave, wisely doing "what is just and right in the land" (Jer 23:5). Also in our country there are deficiencies. What can you do in your not so perfect situation? "Thy Kingdom come!"

 ITH an everlasting love I have loved you; therefore I have continued My mercy toward you. — Jer 31:3

JUNE 23

Learning to Be Merciful

Life is that ongoing interplay of ups and downs. Jeremiah is known best for his emphasis on the downs. We even speak of an endless jeremiad! We are sinners who deserve punishment if we don't repent. But when we do, Jeremiah assures us, God is ready to forgive and take us back with love: "There is hope for your future, says the Lord" (Jer 31:17).

Gratefully think of this and apply it to those "who trespass against us." Can you honestly pray this line in the Lord's Prayer?

95

EARN where there is prudence where there is strength, where there is understanding.   —Bar 3:14

Prudence, Strength, and Understanding

For believers, reason and faith are not more contradictory than reason and love for lovers. Both believers and lovers follow an intuition that should not be unreasonable lest belief becomes superstition and love degenerates into sentimental puppy love.

Not walking along the path of "prudence, strength, and understanding," e.g., neglecting communication, usually precedes drifting away from both the faith and the love commitment. Check your walking!

 HE [prudence] is the book of God's commandments, the law that endures forever.   —Bar 4:1

Avoiding Legalism

Legalism, obeying the law for the law's sake, is a malignancy that plagues many an organized religion. Taking love as the starting point of our ethical thinking may diminish deviations, but we should pay attention to the "book of God's commandments" as well. There is much prudence in it, which keeps our love sane.

With which of the Church's laws do you have trouble and how do you handle it? "Teach me Your way, O Lord, and I will walk in Your truth" (Ps 87:11).

ANIEL resolved not to defile himself with the king's food and wine.

—Dan 1:8

JUNE 26

Preparing Youths to Say No

As Joseph said "no" to Potiphar's wife (Gen 39:8), so Daniel said "no" and obeyed the laws of his religion. Three youths refused to worship a statue and were cast into a furnace (Dan 3:21). Daniel ended up in the lions' den (Dan 6:17ff). God's vindication followed in both cases.

Youths are the product of our education. Love, religion, communication are important— but so is determination. Too soft an education does not prepare youths to say "no" to dope pushers. What about your word and example?

HE fingers of a human hand appeared and wrote on the plaster of the wall near the lampstand in the king's palace. — Dan 5:5

JUNE 27

The Handwriting on the Wall

When the king saw the wrist and hand that wrote, his face blanched, his hip joints shook, and his knees knocked. Daniel explained the handwriting on the wall (Dan 5:5ff).

Nicotine, alcohol, dope, pride, selfishness, and apathy may destroy me. Do I watch that handwriting on the wall? As Christians, we do not have to go through our knees like King Belshazzar, but can be more realistic in our discernment. Moreover, I do not have to cope with the handwriting on the wall by myself. God is with me. Do I turn to Him for help?

WILL espouse you in faithfulness, and you will acknowledge the Lord.

— Hos 2:22

JUNE 28

Repentance and Forgiveness

The prophet Hosea is known for comparing God's faithless people to an adulteress, i.e., his own wife. And just as Hosea eventually took his wife back, so God does not renounce us forever. If I say, "I will go back to my first husband," God is willing to take me back. Then "I [God] will lead her into the desert and speak tenderly to her [through meditation or a good retreat?], and she will respond" (Hos 2:9, 16, 17).

We may pray, "Remember not the sins of my youth . . . in Your kindness remember me" (Ps 25:7). And we shall acknowledge the Lord!

 OUR love is like a morning cloud, like the early dew that disappears.

—Hos 6:4

JUNE 29

Steadfast Love for God

Applied to a marriage, this statement would be disastrous. Is genuine love not supposed to be enduring? But Hosea sees God's people as related to Him in love. God is our spouse!

Check your religious practices, which carry your "love." The prophet has God say, "In their affliction, they will seek Me" (Hos 6:1). Do I need affliction to remain faithful? Neglect and indifference in time of prosperity kill love. Ask for strength and perseverance so that you can pray, "My heart is steadfast, O God" (Ps 108:2).

EPHRAIM is like a dove, silly and without sense. **JUNE**

— Hos 7:11 **30**

Knowing and Praising God

Hosea also says: "When Israel was a child I [God] loved him . . . It was I Who taught Ephraim [one of the tribes] to walk, taking them by the arms; but they did not realize that it was I Who healed them" (Hos 11:1, 3, 4). We are senseless if we do not cultivate a true relationship with our greatest benefactor, Almighty God.

When and where did God bless you recently and how was your response? On Sunday morning, we should make meaningful our statement, "It is right to give Him thanks and praise."

───────────────

THEN afterward I will pour out My Spirit upon all people. **JULY**

—Joel 3:1 **1**

Freedom and Dependence

Contemporary theology is more aware than previously that we don't know how the interaction between total dependence on God as Prime Mover and our own freedom and responsibility should be conceived. I know that "in Him [God]" I "live and move and have [my] being" (Act 17:28), but also that I am a free person, responsible for whatever I do and don't do.

I make my decisions accordingly, and when lacking the stamina to move I pray, "Father of light, . . . by the flame of Your wisdom open the horizons of our minds" (Mass of Pentecost).

AM a shepherd and a dresser of sycamores. . . . The Lord said to me, "Go, prophesy to My people Israel." — Am 7:14-15

JULY 2

Taking Correction Graciously

Amos comes through as a boorish prophet. He was of humble origin and had his gripes against the rich. In the royal sanctuary of Bethel he preached on social justice, "Hear this word, . . . , you women who oppress the poor and abuse the needy" (Am 4:1). Small wonder that the priest told him to go: "Off with you, seer" (Am 7:12).

Can I stand to be corrected by anyone—children, students, or coworkers? "Wisdom opened the mouths of the dumb and loosened the tongues of infants" (Wis 10:21). Check and repent!

 ET I [Jesus] must continue on My way today, tomorrow, and the next day. — Lk 13:33

JULY 3

Christ's Salvific Dedication

The sacred writers see Jesus dying on the cross as a Jewish High Priest offering bloody sacrifice to atone for sins! (See May 15.) We should realize that salvation was brought to us by Christ's dedication to His call, which led to a death that He did not dodge (see Lk 13:31).

Our call in life is not always rewarding! Being aware that Jesus intercedes for us (Rom 8:34; Heb 7:25) and praying ourselves for courage to faithfully continue our way as Jesus did is salvific. God hears prayers!

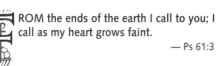

FROM the ends of the earth I call to you; I call as my heart grows faint.

— Ps 61:3

JULY
4

Dependence and Freedom

The mystery of being dependent on God and yet free and responsible for our actions has puzzled theologians over the centuries. Both dependency and freedom are data of faith. We must avoid pitfalls on either side. Both taking it too easy and arrogantly defying God by seizing the wheel in your own hands are wrong.

Whatever our achievements are, we must still humbly pray, "Not to us, O Lord, not to us but to Your name be the glory" (Ps 115:1). And by all means call to God.

THE kingdom of the world has become the kingdom of our Lord and His Anointed, and He will reign forever.

— Rev 11:15

JULY
5

An Everlasting Reign

God is the source of all life. Why then is there so much pain, frustration, injustice, and discord in human history? Apocalyptic expectations, a utopian longing for the end of human misery and the coming of a reign of peace, have popped up time and again. The Book of Revelation shows us the background of this mystery: Jesus and His movement! We believe that He will come again, but we don't know when.

When depressed, pray for faith and perseverance. Think of Handel's immortal Hallelujah. Chorus: "He will reign for ever and ever!"

REPENT, for the Kingdom of Heaven [i.e., God] is at hand!

— Mt 3:2

The Coming of God's Kingdom

Both John the Baptist and Jesus preach repentance, because the kingdom, i.e., God's reign, His triumph over evil and death, is at hand (see Mt 4:17). For John, it is ushered in by a judgment in which sinners will perish. In Christian understanding, God's reign is anticipated now and will culminate in Jesus' second coming.

In order to be part of it, constant reform of self is mandatory. "Prepare the way of the Lord!" (Mt 3:3). Do so by realizing God's reign in and around you by love and concern!

JESUS came from Galilee to the Jordan to be baptized by John.

— Mt 3:13

The Baptism of Jesus

His baptism by John was a profound disclosure experience for Jesus. Perhaps it caused a first awareness of His own call as a prophet (see Mt 3:16-17). By His baptism, He may have intended to tell Israel that it needed conversion. By an explanatory vision, the Gospels have interpreted it as such: "This is My beloved Son. Listen to Him!" (Mt 3:17; 17:5).

What about a first awareness of your call as a baptized Christian, spouse, religious, or priest? What about growth and perseverance? Pray for guidance, and if necessary repent!

OUR kingdom come!
— Mt 6:10

God's Loving Presence

Jesus' central message is the Kingdom (reign) of God, by which He means a dynamic awareness of God's loving presence, a situation of well-being. There are demands (He reigns!), but they are requirements of love—which may not always result in fun but certainly guarantee lasting happiness.

God's reign is "good news." It is the generous love of God that has appeared (see Tit 3:4). Be grateful for being part of it, and whenever you say the Lord's Prayer ask that God's reign may come and be experienced ever more by all.

———————

AX collectors and prostitutes are entering the Kingdom of God ahead of you.
— Mt 21:31

JULY

9

Entry into the Kingdom

Although the Kingdom of God is one of our Lord's most beloved metaphors, He nowhere explains it clearly. We learn what it means from His preaching, parables, and life-style.

Tax collectors (loan sharks today?) and prostitutes enter before those who pay lip service only. Our Lord is not interested in our past. He loves us as we are. Faith, change of mind, and repentance, though, are the requirements for entering the kingdom (see Mt 21:30-32). "Create in me a clean heart, O God" (Ps 51:12).

ROM the days of John the Baptist until now, the Kingdom of Heaven has been forcefully advancing, and the forceful are taking hold of it by storm. — Mt 11:12

Growth of God's Kingdom in Us

There was continuity in the message about the Kingdom of God preached by John the Baptist and by Jesus—both preached repentance. But there was a profound breach as well—not God's wrath but His mercy is final. The power of the kingdom was manifested in Jesus' works, His miraculous healings (Lk 7:21-23).

As for the growth of God's kingdom in you, there may be forces (peer pressure, shows, life-style, literature) that paralyze it. You may have to make a painful choice. Pray for strength.

ET the least person in the Kingdom of Heaven is greater than he.

— Mt 11:11

Benefits of the Kingdom

Although there was a breach between the movement of Jesus and that of John, Jesus never made that difference of opinion personal: "Among those born of women, none is greater than John" (Lk 7:28). But to be in the kingdom is so great a privilege that the least in it is greater than the Baptist (Mt 11:11).

By faith and Baptism we are in God's kingdom. Does your life-style reflect your appreciation? Can you disagree agreeably? "My heart trusts in Him, and I find help; then . . . I give thanks to Him in song" (Ps 28:7).

ESUS went throughout Galilee, teaching in their synagogues, proclaiming the gospel of the kingdom, and healing every disease and infirmity among the people. —Mt 4:23

JULY 12

Practicing Works of Charity

For Jesus, healing and consoling go with preaching the good news of God's kingdom. We Christians should preach the good news in the same fashion: "But you, go and proclaim the Kingdom of God" (Lk 9:60). Forget burying your father or saying good-bye to your family (see Lk 9:57-62)—sayings that indicate the unconditional nature of Christian discipleship.

Check your priority of values! Are you involved in any charity work of your church? What could be your prayerful answer?

UT the subjects of the kingdom will be driven outside into the darkness. —Mk 8:12

JULY 13

Importance of a Right Intention

The kingdom as brought to perfection is compared to a banquet. The Jewish patriarchs recline, but the Israelites who refuse to believe in Jesus are rejected. Jesus healed the centurion's servant (a pagan) because of his faith.

What counts with God is not your status in the parish or even your charitable activities unless they were motivated by faith and love. Do you ever do the right thing for the wrong reason? Check and pray for an increase of faith!

105

OT everyone who says to Me, "Lord, Lord," will enter the Kingdom of Heaven, but only the one who does the will of My Father. — Mt

JULY 14

Genuine Religion

All organized religion knows members who pay lip service only. Daily Mass attendance, novenas, lighted candles, and donations don't guarantee you will be "in that number when the saints go marching in," unless all of it is followed up by an honest Christian life of love."

What counts is the reason why you are religious and charitable. It would be bad if our Lord should say to you, "I never knew you" (Mt 7:23), because of your lack of genuine love. Lord, help me to do it honestly!

 [JESUS] will give you [Peter] the keys to the Kingdom of Heaven.

—Mt 16:19

JULY 15

The Keeper of the Keys

Here, "kingdom" means the community established by God's reign, practically synonymous with Church. However, kingdom and Church are not identical. Since Vatican II we are ever more aware that "the Kingdom of God" is prepared for in all people of goodwill.

Peter, hence the Pope, has a special position of authority in the Church. As members of the family, we should be loyal. Pray for faith to be so and have an open eye for the signs of God's kingdom wherever you encounter truth, love, and goodwill.

WHO is the greatest in the Kingdom of Heaven? . . . Unless you . . . become like children, you will never enter the kingdom. — Mt 18:1-3

Accepting Ourselves as We Are

Ego boosting may be done by buying a luxury car or a TV set larger than the one next door. Showing oneself as a VIP by "having" is easier than by "being"—the way the Lord suggests: humbling oneself like a child (Mt 18:4).

Humility means accepting yourself as you are with your limitations, which may be social, intellectual, religious, and whatever comes with aging, aware of your total dependence on God, like a child on his/her parents. "Lord, help me to be just myself, not less and not more!"

LET the little children come to Me, and do not hinder them; for the Kingdom of Heaven belongs to such as these.
—Mt 19:14

Making Allowance for Children

I was once reproved for paying a substantial gas bill for an unwed mother with three children. "The more you help, the more irresponsible she gets!" But what about those children who did not ask for life? Let them freeze? I was told to get after the children who steal pecans from my trees. But as an altar boy I myself stole apples from the yard of my pastor!

All of us should never forget that we were once children. Our Lord laid hands on them and prayed (Mt 19:13). So should we.

T will be hard for such a person to enter the Kingdom of Heaven.

—Mt 19:23

False Security

Having money, youth, and health generates false security. Our Lord does not require that all Christians take a vow of poverty, neither does He object to providing security for self and family. What He rejects is false security, lack of final dependence on God. Regardless of your bank account, you are only God's caretaker.

Awareness of this will make you share generously with God's poor and create the attitude needed to enter the kingdom and achieve salvation as a gift of God. Pray for true security!

RANT that one of these two sons of mine may sit at Your right and the other at Your left, in Your kingdom.

— Mt 20:21

Greatness Means Humble Service

"Sitting next to the king" is a Hebrew idiom for "sharing his power, splendor, and wealth." Greatness in the Kingdom of God is not lordly power but humble service. Not only members of the hierarchy should realize this but also church workers. Jesus says, "High officials make their authority over their subject felt. It shall not be so among you" (Mt 20:25-26).

How do you handle authority in the family, on your job, in church work? Are you always aware that you are dealing with unique human beings? Pray for guidance!

ETTER for you to enter the Kingdom of God with one eye than to have two eyes and be thrown into Gehenna.

—Mk 9:47

No Room for Compromise!

Human as we are, we are constantly tempted not to live up to our Christian call. Lowering standards is a dreadful process that often comes with aging. It is one of the reasons business sidetracks senior employees and even the Church makes bishops retire at seventy-five.

Anticipating God's reign on this side of the grave requires determination. There can be no lowering of standards in any commitment of love. In the Kingdom of God there is no room for compromise. Constantly pray for the stamina to keep moving!

 EEK His kingdom, and these things will be given to you as well.

— Lk 12:31

A Right Priority of Values

In our country the work ethic is highly valued. We are supposed to earn whatever we need. We know that the ravens do not sow, the flowers do not toil or spin, and my heavenly Father knows what I need (see Lk 12:22-34), but I still have to pay my bills. The answer is to strike a balance. Do what you can and then trust God!

"Your Father is pleased to give you the kingdom." Ask for guidance and create a right priority of values, "for where your treasure is, there your heart will also be" (Lk 12:32-34).

O one can enter the Kingdom of God unless he is born of water and the Spirit. — Jn 3:5

Water and the Spirit

Baptism, the first phase of Christian initiation (Eucharist and Confirmation follow) is seen as a birth: "from above" (see Jn 3:1-5). Water, fire, and blowing wind are apt symbols, which approach the mystery of God's presence in us (see Acts 2:1-13). Without God's Spirit motivating us, flesh is just flesh and we are not fully alive (see Jn 3:6). We are part of Christ's worldwide movement, the Kingdom of God.

Veterans proudly display their medals of honor. Word and example should show our Christian dignity. "Come, Holy Spirit. . . ."

 TELL you that the Kingdom of God will be taken away from you and given to a people who will produce its fruit. — Mt 21:43

Exercising Faithful Stewardship

I have listened to prison inmates recounting how they had ruined their lives. One told me a few hours before his execution, "I must die. Will you give this ring to my wife?" Matthew is hard on those who hesitate to make a definitive commitment.

Am I exercising faithful stewardship over what God has entrusted to me, the gift of Faith included? Let's not wait until it's too late before "producing" in word and example. "God, help me to grow in the Faith and produce fruit as I should."

ND this gospel of the kingdom will be preached throughout the whole world as a testimony to all nations.
— Mt 24:14

JULY 24

The Power of Example

Mahatma Ghandi, the devout Hindu freedom fighter, carried the Gospels with him wherever he went. He admired Jesus. Allegedly, he had said, "If I would not have seen in Europe how Christians actually live, I would be a Christian." In his eyes, Christians did not preach the Gospel of the kingdom by their life-style!

What about your church's priority of values? Do the poor feel welcome? Is the issue of social justice ever brought up? On your job, does your behavior make coworkers think?

NHERIT the kingdom prepared for you from the foundation of the world.
—Mt 25:34

JULY 25

Accepting Jesus in Others

In Mt 25, 31-46, we read how Jesus identifies with the least of His brothers and sisters. Over the three decades that I have been serving black congregations, insensitive whites have more than once made derogatory remarks about blacks in my presence. My reactions have not always been patient. Insulting my black friends hurts me! Similarly, Jesus expects us to accept His brothers and sisters and be worthy to inherit the kingdom.

Are all Catholics in your congregation also Christians? "Lord, help me to be a Christian in the Catholic tradition!"

BLESSED is the one who eats bread in the Kingdom of God.
— Lk 14:15

Constantly Check Your Priorities

A sound philosophy of life, conducive to a meaningful and happy existence, implies a right priority of values. In Lk 14:15-24, many who were invited to a dinner party found business and sex reasons to decline. Fun gives instant gratification. Work can be the pretense not to spend enough time with spouse and children, and the busy sister-social worker may have no time for prayer and community life.

Check your priority of values constantly with God's invitation in mind! "[Lord], guard my life and save me" (Ps 25:20).

———————

CONFER a kingdom on you . . . that you may eat and drink at My table in My kingdom.
— Lk 22:29-30

Greatness Consists in Service

Jesus promises His disciples, who were arguing about who of them should be regarded as the greatest, that they will eat and drink at His table in His kingdom if they comply with His philosophy that greatness consists in service. Kings of past times and cultures were endowed with absolute power for life. Jesus said, "Among you it shall not be like that! . . . Let the greatest be as the . . . one who serves" (Lk 22:26).

What about service in your family, religious community, and church? You want to sit at the Lord's table. Pray for humility.

THEY believed Philip as he preached the good news about the Kingdom of God.
— Act 8:12

Sharing the Good News

When there is good news, say another grandchild born into the extended family, doesn't grandma get on the phone and share it? Convinced that "the Kingdom of God" is good news, the disciples of Jesus shared it.

Preaching is no longer the exclusive task of priests. Competent religious and lay persons conduct retreats and Bible prayer groups, and are the soul of our Church schools. No matter what we do, all of us should share the "good news" by our joyful word and behavior.

HE [Paul] entered the synagogue, and for three months debated boldly, arguing persuasively about the Kingdom of God.
— Act 19:8

Scholarship and Intuition

Handbooks for Bible study groups now stress experience and feeling. In the realm of Faith and love the intuitive is of paramount importance. But just as love without reason becomes puppy love, so Faith without persuasive arguments becomes fideism.

We need both scholarship and intuition. This meditation book tries to offer both. Do you complete your meditations on the "good news of the kingdom" always with prayer that comes from both heart and mind?

HE Kingdom of God does not consist in food and drink, but in righteousness, peace, and joy in the Holy Spirit. —Rom 14:17

JULY 30

Focusing on Essentials

In a cathedral I spied an old woman devoutly kneeling and fingering the rosary. Is there something wrong with this sort of devotion? No, unless a Mass is being celebrated at the same time—which it was. Every so often devotees in organized religion deviate from essentials.

Paul is dealing with Jewish Christians who wish to have dietary laws observed by non-Jewish Christians. Let us focus on the essentials, which Paul mentions above, without judging others who may act differently (Rom 14:13).

 LESH and blood cannot inherit the Kingdom of God, nor does corruption inherit incorruption. —1 Cor 15:50

JULY 31

The Resurrected Body

With Paul's parishioners in Corinth, we too may ask, "With what kind of body will the dead [rise]?" (1 Cor 15:35). Paul does not give an adequate answer. We may observe that the molecules that serve me at the moment of death return to where they came from.

But I, in continuity with the person I made of myself with God's help and who is never entirely without "body" in Hebrew thought, will be incorruptible and happy with God. "In the Lord your labor is not in vain" (1 Cor 15:58).

LL this is evidence that God's judgment is just, so that you may be accounted worthy of the Kingdom of God for which you are suffering.

— 2 Thes 1:5

Suffering for the Kingdom

The Thessalonians were willing to endure afflictions for the sake of the kingdom because they found it worthwhile (2 Thes 1:4). Enslavement to any evil hurts you as the person God designed you to be.

Only if you see enslavement to evil as hurting and the kingdom as precious can you be willing to "suffer" for it. Is any evil keeping you captive? "God, open my eyes and strengthen my will!"

E who are receiving the unshakable kingdom should be grateful and thus offer acceptable worship to God in reverence and awe.

— Heb 12:28

Praise and Gratitude

The "unshakable kingdom" is the metaphor that covers whatever the "good news" comprises. Does lack of gratitude originate from lack of reflective meditation on God's gift?

God does not owe a thing to me who am transient on spaceship "Earth." Yet He knows me, loves me, and is constantly concerned about me. "It is right to give Him thanks and praise" (Preface at Mass). Make it your prayer when worshiping next Sunday!

ID not God choose those who are poor in the world to be rich in faith and to inherit the kingdom that He promised to those who love Him? — Jas 2:5

Option for the Poor

Nowadays, the "option for the poor" is a frequent topic of discussion in Church documents. There are still Catholics who are afraid of doing what James encouraged the rich to do in chapter 2 of his letter. Yet giving the poor handouts, as the Church has done over the centuries, is not the same as changing political structures and accepting the poor as equal partners.

God chooses the poor. What do you, your parish council, and the representatives you vote for do in this regard?

———

T is through the Holy Spirit that this Child has been conceived in her.

—Mt 1:20

Conceived through the Spirit

By both his genealogy (1:1-17) and his report on Mary's unusual pregnancy, Matthew depicts Jesus as a very important person, the son of David, leader of God's people, to be called Jesus, i.e., "Yahweh helps and saves." Moreover, conceived "through the holy Spirit," Jesus is so intimately one with God that He is "Emmanuel—God-with-us," assuring us that we don't have to go it alone (see 1:23).

Your meditation on what Jesus means to us (leader, savior, Emmanuel) may result in a prayerful response of thanksgiving!

OSEPH [Mary's] husband, since he was a righteous man and unwilling to expose her to shame, decided to send her away quietly. — Mt 1:19

AUG. 5

Innocent till Proven Guilty

In Biblical culture, marriage was arranged by the parents often right after the age of puberty. The girl stayed with her parents and sex was permitted only after final adjustments had been made. Now Mary was pregnant! Joseph is called "righteous," perfectly in accord with Jewish law by intending to divorce her. His greatness is that he wants to do it "quietly."

"Innocent till proven guilty" is the law of our land. If we are inclined to be judgmental, we can learn from Joseph!

 IVE Your servant . . . a discerning heart to judge Your people and to distinguish between right and wrong. — 1 Ki 3:9

AUG. 6

Pristine Devotion

King Solomon did not ask for a long life, nor for riches, nor for the life of his enemies (1 Ki 3:11). He was an idealistic young man! Growing older, however, he did not persevere.

How did you start out? Think of the early days of your marriage, your religious life, your priesthood. "When Solomon was old . . . his heart was not fully devoted to the Lord" (1 Ki 11:4). Jeremiah has God say, "I remember the devotion of your youth, how as a bride you loved Me" (2:2). Reflect and pray!

E faithful to the Lord all the days of your life, my son. . . . Avoid all forms of immorality. . . . — Tob 4:5, 12

Parental Advice

Tobit advises his son. Parents are responsible for their children, advising them from early infancy on by word and example, lovingly but firmly as well. Details are up to parents of every time and culture. Loving children without spoiling them is basic.

And all adults must feel responsible. Church school teachers, youth leaders, and everyone involved in education are priceless helps. What is your particular responsibility?

———————

UR paschal lamb, Christ, has been sacrificed. — 1 Cor 5:7

Celebrating the Eucharist

Jesus is the "Lamb of God" Who takes away the sins of the world. In Jewish cult, the Passover is followed by the feast of the Unleavened Bread. Hence, calling to mind Jesus' death, resurrection, and ascension into heaven and our own passage from death to life with Him, we must do away with the yeast (old dough!) of malice and wickedness and celebrate every Eucharist with the unleavened bread of sincerity and truth (see 1 Cor 5:6-8).

"God, may we become one body, one spirit in Christ."

THE healthy do not need a physician, but the sick do.

—Mk 2:17

The Divine Physician

The scribes criticized Jesus for eating with tax collectors and sinners. Jewish institutional law made members who did so unclean. Jesus, though, considers himself a physician.

Only when you feel ill do you make an appointment with your doctor. What are your weak spots as a Christian? Being self-righteous, you are like a woman who delays a recommended cancer smear till it is too late. Pray with Jeremiah: "Heal me, O Lord, that I may be healed. Save me!" (Jer 17:14).

IF salt loses its taste, what can it be seasoned with?

—Mt 5:13

The Salt of the Earth

Before the time of freezers and refrigerators, salt was the means used to preserve food. We Christians are the prophetical element in the world, trying to preserve it from the corruption of evil: "You are the salt of the earth" (Mt 5:13).

Depravity may come at us from many sources. Check what tears you down and where you fail in the field of loving God and neighbor. Be aware that if we fail, we are no longer good for anything, like salt, but to be thrown out (Mt 5:13). "I confess to Almighty God . . . that I have sinned."

UT they [the parents of Jesus] did not understand.

— Lk 2:50

The Anxiety of Parents

Without telling His parents, Jesus remained behind in Jerusalem. After they had found Him, Mary said to Jesus, "Son, why have You done this to us?" (Lk 2:48). Jesus' answer does not explain why He had not told His parents first.

I observe in Mary's question the same anxiety that so many parents of teenagers go through. "Is my son or daughter in college doing all right?" Pray for parents to learn from Mary and Joseph, and be grateful to your own parents who guided you through your difficult years.

 ND Jesus advanced in wisdom and age and grace before God and man.

— Lk 2:52

Advancing in Grace

After the painful incident in the temple of Jerusalem, Jesus went home with His parents, and He "advanced." We should never feel too old to keep "advancing" in wisdom and grace before God and human beings. We all know selfish old people who did not advance. Children shun them. And we are acquainted with lovable old men and women. Instinctively kids love them, and adults share in their wisdom.

In which category do you want to be a few years from now? Don't wait with "advancing," and pray to your Maker to help you.

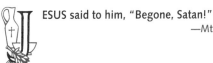 ESUS said to him, "Begone, Satan!"

—Mt 4:10

AUG.

13

Handling Temptations

Matthew describes Jesus' temptations with those of all humans in mind. The way to handle them is through determination and the awareness that obedience to God, your Father, is characteristic of your status as God's child.

In the narrative, Jesus answers Satan with quotes from the Bible. Would you be able to do the same? Or do you know certain movie stars and sports heroes better than the great people of the Bible, including the Lord Jesus Who was tempted like you and me? Work and pray for deliverance from temptation.

 E said to them "Follow Me.

—Mt 4:19

AUG.

14

Called to Follow Christ

All of us are called in life to become the kind of person our Maker has designed us to be. For Christians, this means to "follow" Christ, since He is our God-given model to imitate. This call implies ministering to others in His name.

Today, in addition to the full-time ministry of priests, new ministries are appearing in the Church. What are the ones in your parish? Be responsive to the call, "Follow Me." Make time and be no less dedicated than the first Apostles in your own way (see Mt 4:18-22).

121

LL who heard it were amazed by what the shepherds told them.

—Lk 2:18

AUG.
15

The Value of Amazement

Amazement is an element in love and in faith as well. It is an intuitive surmise where there is no certain evidence as yet. Simple people are easier amazed than the sophisticated. Perhaps that's why they are more able to love!

We can learn a few things from the country folk in Luke's story and from Mary too. "Mary kept all these things, pondering on them in her heart" (Lk 2:19). Do it prayerfully: "Amazing grace! how sweet the sound, that saved and set me free. I once was lost, but now am found, was blind, but now I see."

OU have heard that it was said, "An eye for an eye. . . ." But I [Christ] tell you, do not resist an evil person.

—Mt 5:38-39

AUG.
16

Non-Resistance Not Vengeance

Jesus tells us to offer no resistance to one who is evil. He refuses to endorse the moderate vengeance of the law of talion—an eye for an eye—which decreed that the punishment could not exceed the injury done. For the Christian, even proportionate retaliation is forbidden.

Self-defense is permitted, but we should not take the law into our own hands. Pray for courage to imitate our Lord. When arrested, He did not agree with the person who cut off the ear of the high priest's servant (see Mt 26:51).

FOR if you love those who love you, what reward will you get?

— Mt 5:46

AUG.
17

Loving without Self-Interest

If you greet only your brothers and sisters, what is unusual about that? Do not the non-Christians do the same (Mt 6:47)? Jesus challenges us to do the unusual. Visiting an aged aunt in the nursing home is all right. But what about asking the social worker for names of a few of the most abandoned and lonely old people and visiting them every so often? Unusual? Yes, but a Christian challenge.

Pray for the courage to be perfect, "just as your heavenly Father is perfect" (Mt 5:48).

WHEN you pray, go to your room, close the door and pray to your Father, Who is unseen.

— Mt 6:6

AUG.
18

Making Time for Prayer

As you may have noticed in the Preface, this book is written for busy people who may not have time to go to their "room" for extended prayer. I hope and pray that using it may eventually lead you to make time.

I wrote my book *Bible Meditations for Every Day* (see inside back cover) for you "in your room with the door closed!" You need quiet for concentration and to grow in awareness of the divine in you. What is your priority of values? Ask the Lord to teach you "to pray" (see Lk 11:1).

123

ND forgive us our sins, for we ourselves also forgive everyone who is
indebted to us.   — Lk 11:4

AUG.
19

Forgive and Be Forgiven

The Lord's Prayer as finally authorized for
Church use has the words "And forgive us our
trespasses as we forgive those who trespass
against us." In Luke it reads, "for we ourselves also forgive everyone who is indebted
to us." It presupposes that those who say the
prayer do forgive their debtors. May that be
the case with us!

In Matthew, Jesus adds, "If you do not forgive
others their trespasses, neither will your Father
forgive [you]" (Mt 6:15). What about your broken relationships and receiving Communion?

SK, and it will be given to you.

—Mt 7:7

AUG.
20

Hoping against Hope

His twenty-year-old son survived the car
wreck and finally emerged from the coma, but
he will be demented and crippled for life. The
desperate father exclaimed to me, "I thought
God hears our prayers. Now I don't know. If He
exists, what kind of God is He?" The theological answer is, "How much more will your heavenly Father give good things to those who ask
Him" (Mt 7: 11). But you must let Him decide
what is good for you!

It is not easy. Even Jesus on the cross exclaimed, "My God, why have You forsaken
Me?" (Mt 26:39). Yet we must prayerfully try.

124

VERYONE who hears these words of Mine and carries them out will be like a wise man who built his house on rock.
—Mt 7:24

Heeding the Words of the Lord

After the fatal space shuttle accident, more tests are conducted than ever before. "The rains fell, the floods came, and the winds blew and beat upon the house" (Mt 7:25). Tests are necessary to find out whether or not we have been building on rock. Does your philosophy of life withstand the tests?

Listen to the Lord's words in your Bible and act on them; otherwise you are like a fool who built his house on sand (see Mt 7:26).

HY does your teacher eat with tax collectors and sinners?
—Mt 9:11

Table Fellowship

The answer to the above question is well known. "The healthy do not need a physician, but the sick do" (Mt 9:12). At a banquet, fellowship with the host, hostess, and participating guests is more important than the food that is served. When we participate in the Eucharist, we are invited to enjoy table fellowship with the risen Lord.

Are we aware that we need healing from sin? "May all of us who share in the body and blood of Christ be brought together in unity by the Holy Spirit" (Eucharistic Prayer III).

AKE heart, daughter! Your faith has saved you. — Mt 9:22

The Healing Power of Faith

Meditating on the healing accounts in the, Bible, we should keep in mind that the background of these stories is prescientific. Sickness and early death were regarded as punishment for sin. Demons and evil spirits had something to do with suffering and pain.

The authors edited traditions that had been circulating and fashioned them to bring out their point, namely the healing presence of God in the Lord Jesus and the importance of faith in order to share in it. Pray for the faith of that "daughter": "If only I can touch His cloak, I shall be made well" (Mt 9:21).

ESUS went around all the cities and villages, teaching . . . , proclaiming the gospel of the kingdom, and healing.
— Mk 9:35

Christ's Threefold Concern

Our Lord's motivation for his activities was pity for the crowds, because they were troubled and abandoned (Mt 9:36). His heart is still moved with pity for you and for me. The Gospel of the kingdom should encourage us when we are depressed. The Lord's teaching is available when we need direction. The Lord's healing is ever present to overcome our bad habits through confession and prayerful dialogue.

Expose yourself to our Lord's threefold concern in meditative prayer.

B E wise as serpents and simple as doves. **AUG.**
— Mt 10:16

25

The Virtue of Simplicity

Academics ask questions; that's what they are trained to do. This does not mean that they must become agnostics, going to church only to keep the family together. By combining "wisdom" with "simplicity, that is, the ability to love, they can appreciate the mysteries of faith through intuition.

Without intuition, both love and faith go down the drain. An infra-red light detector may discover ancient galaxies but cannot uncover what is wrong with a person's love or faith life! Pray: "Lord, keep me able to both love and believe!"

C OME to Me, all you who labor and **AUG.**
are burdened, and I will give you
rest. — Mk 11:28

26

Christ Our Refuge

As a doctor under stress, a friend of mine often goes to the woods to hunt, fish, and just to sit in a tree at night watching the stars. God crosses his mind every so often. Finding rest for yourself is important (see Mt 11:29).

Sitting in a tree at night may not be your cup of tea. It is not mine either! But turning to Christ in meditative prayer is a must for me to keep sane. I hope that it is also for you. There is sound wisdom in the Bible. Be grateful that we have it available in the Christian tradition.

THE Kingdom of Heaven is like yeast that a woman took and mixed with three measures of wheat flour.

— Mt 13:33

We Should Be Like Yeast

The only thing most of us still remember about yeast is that it has an uplifting impact, invisible, slow but steady. The parable teaches that the Kingdom of Heaven will affect many people (the "three measures of wheat"). It does so today through its members like you and me.

Do your behavior and your conversation on the job have an uplifting impact? Or do you follow the common trend of gossip and loveless remarks? Pray, "Hear the sound of my cry . . ." (Ps 28:2-3).

HEN he found a pearl of great price, he went away and sold all that he had and bought it.

— Mt 13:46

The Pearl of Great Price

In 1987, "The Irises," a painting by Vincent Van Gogh, was sold for 49 million dollars. What motivated the buyer to pay that amount? During this century, thousands of young people gave up the founding of a happy family, left their homelands, and went off to preach the Kingdom of God far away. What motivated them? Is the kingdom so precious a pearl?

In order to sacrifice for something, you must find it precious and be determined to obtain it. Do you find Christ's philosophy of life precious enough to "sell" a few things and buy it?

128

HOEVER wishes to come after Me must deny himself, take up his cross, and follow Me.

AUG.
29

—Mt 16:24

The Cost of Discipleship

Shortly before he was executed for his Christian Faith, Dietrich Bonhoeffer, a German Lutheran minister, wrote a book, *The Cost of Discipleship*. He practiced Jesus' words, "Whoever loses his life for My sake will find it" (Mt 16:25). Such Christian living requires faith! Peter said to Jesus, "Even if I should have to die with You, I will not deny You" (Mt 26:35). But that very night he did deny Christ!

Check where you are tempted to compromise and pray for faith to persevere. It is not easy!

———————

 NO longer call you servants, because a servant does not know what his master is doing. Instead, I have called you friends.

AUG.
30

—Jn 15:15

A Relationship of Friendship

How come so many people refuse to accept the message of Jesus as *glad* tidings? The reason is that many of us do not experience our relationship with God sufficiently as friendship. An employer expects no friendship from an employee—only a good job. The other way around, no friendship but a paycheck is expected.

Jesus does not want this sort of business relationship with you and me. Check your religious motivations! Let love guide you, and the Lord's joy will be in you (see Jn 15:11).

WILL not leave you as orphans; I will come to you. —Jn 14:18

True Riches

When a rich man falls in love with a poor young woman, she will soon be poor no longer. She will wear expensive clothes and jewelry and drive a good car. We are poor, and we don't deserve an intimate relationship of love with God. But He wants it! "Realize that I am in My Father and you are in Me and I in you" (Jn 14:20).

That closeness of God is our richness. Jesus did not leave us as orphans. Right now He thinks of you and me. Respond in love and foster the awareness of God's closeness to you.

OR it is written in the Book of Psalms: . . . "Let another take his office."

—Act 1:20

Faults of Christ's Representatives

The problem of "human" ministers already troubled the early Church. Judas betrayed the Master, and Peter denied Him three times. Should we, therefore, do away with our ministers and their authority? Not at all! We need them as an alternative to chaos. Another person took Judas' office, and a repentant Peter was given a second chance.

Be aware that our chief minister is the Lord Jesus. Priests, bishops, and popes are only His human representatives. Pray for them and do not let defaults shake your faith and dedication.

NOW, therefore, and fix in your heart, that the Lord is God . . . , and there is no other. —Deut 4:39

SEPT. 2

Putting God above All Others

The Bible stresses that we are related to God in an intimate bond of marital love: "For the Lord takes delight in you and makes your land [you!] His spouse" (Isa 62:4); "God is love" (1 Jn 4:16). And we are invited to love Him: "You shall love the Lord your God with all your heart" (Mk 12:30).

Hence, when I love idols like wealth (having), pleasure (time spent on . . .), or power (being bossy) too much, I am unfaithful. Prayerfully check, "Is my love for everyone and the material compatible with my love for God?"

 O not be amazed that I told you, "You must be born again." — Jn 3:7

SEPT. 3

Children of God

God has invested His life, His wisdom (Son), and His love (Holy Spirit) in us. John speaks of "born again" (Jn 3:4), Paul of "adoption" (Rom 8:14-17). By faith and Baptism we became God's children. As a parent, He is interested in how we are doing. Are we becoming the persons He expects us to be for eternity?

Nicodemus asked Jesus, "How can this be?" Jesus mentions faith (Jn 3:9-12). Pray for faith and appreciation and the determination not to "drop out" of the school that life is.

E are always full of courage, . . . for we live by faith, not by sight.
—2 Cor 5:6-7

SEPT. 4

Living by Faith

In dense fog, a pilot lands his plane by radar, not by sight. But he must be familiar with and trust the system. Faith, an intuition or experience, is a gift like a sense of humor or an ear for music. It can be developed, however, like a pilot's familiarity with radar.

We should pray for an increase of faith and practice "living by faith." Think of things that you believe at which unbelievers raise eyebrows. Are we underprivileged or are they?

OR they did not yet understand the Scripture that He had to rise from the dead.
—Jn 20:9

SEPT. 5

The Empty Tomb

The author depicts three witnesses who see the empty tomb, a woman and two men. None of them readily accepts the resurrection of our Lord. Mary of Magdala runs off. Peter enters the tomb, but there is no indication that he believes. The other disciple goes in, sees, and believes. Only one goes beyond seeing into the personal commitment we call fidelity.

We share the disclosure experience of the early group. The firmer we are in our commitment the easier we can accept those who do not understand. We should not judge them but prayerfully bear witness by word and example.

OMEONE asked Him, "Lord, will those who are saved be few?"

— Lk 13:23

SEPT.

6

Thinking of God

I remember a poster with a montage of pictures: a playing child—"too young to think of God"; a young fellow on a motorbike—"too self-assured to think of God"; a newlywed couple—"too happy to think of God"; a man at a desk—"too busy to think of God"; a woman in bed—"too tired to think of God"; and a tombstone—"too late to think of God."

Luke's Gospel is "good news," but realistically we should read all of it and prayerfully apply it to our own situation. If there is love, there is always time. Check your prayer life!

 ESUS . . . said, "What do you want Me to do for you?" They said to Him, "Lord, we want to see." — Mt 20:32-33

SEPT.

7

In Time of Suffering

Just before this healing account, Jesus predicts His passion for the third time, but the disciples are blind to it all. As the blind men's eyes were opened, so would the disciples' sight be restored as well—after the resurrection.

"In pity, Jesus touched their eyes" (Mt 20:33). When we are in pain, we may be helped to endure it by the awareness that someone is touching us with pity and showing at least some reason why. Can you share this with a friend who suffers? (See Mt 16:21-28; 17:22).

AVE you never read the text, "Out of the mouths of children and infants You have brought perfect praise"?
— Mt 21:16

Serving at the Altar

When I proposed that men should not only read in church but also serve at the altar, I ran into opposition: "That's for boys!" I countered, "If the activities around the altar are just 'kid-stuff,' next Sunday little David Jones will celebrate Mass, and I'll be out fishing." We now have no problem!

Yet we must keep something of a child's dependence on a higher power alive in us. Actively participating in the Liturgy enhances adulthood in its true perspective. Pray for insight!

OU shall love the Lord your God. . . . You shall love your neighbor as yourself.
— Mt 22:37-39

Love of God and Neighbor

Christianity as such depends on these two commandments, and we must constantly return to them. You start with yourself. Without loving yourself as a precious creature of God, you cannot love—period. As yourself, you love your neighbor and in him/her God.

The Bible stresses the totality of love: with all your heart, soul, and mind! There is much lukewarm love. What about yours? Check where you fail. Pray for an increase of love and generosity.

WHY do you trouble the woman? She has done something good for Me. — Mt 26:10

The Most Loving Thing

The disciples regarded pouring costly oil on Jesus' head as wasting money that could have been given to the poor. Jesus disagrees, "Let her alone. She has done what she could" (Mk 14:6, 8). "The poor you always have with you" (Jn 12:8).

Whatever the case, each of us should do the most loving thing in his/her own situation. And love goes by rules and numbers that cannot be calculated by analytic reason alone. "Lord, teach me to love!"

THE Son of Man is going as it is written about Him.

— Mk 14:21

The Mystery of Suffering

Matthew teaches the meaning of our Lord's passion by referring to the Bible's depiction of the suffering just person. Like the suffering of the just, Jesus' pain is also salvific.

Meditating on our Lord's passion and death and referring it to our own pain and frustrations, you should not insist on "why?" Often there is no answer but faith in God, Who has designed this life as a transition to a better one to come. Pray for strength to accept life and its frustrations as Jesus has done. "Your will be done" (Mt 26:39).

men, I say to you, one of you will betray Me.

— Mt 26:21

In the Face of Betrayal

More painful than physical suffering is the betrayal by an allegedly good friend. Both Judas and Peter went wrong. Judas is notorious because he failed to repent. Jesus remains in charge of the situation, "Judas, would you betray the Son of Man with a kiss?" (Lk 22:48).

How do you handle your frustrations with other human beings: spouse, teenagers, friends? There was no outburst of revenge in the Lord Jesus. Pray for strength!

 ARY of Magdala went and told the disciples, "I have seen the Lord," and the things He told her.

— Jn 20:18

Salvation in the Risen Lord

Without the resurrection, to which the early Christians were witnesses, Jesus' life and death would not have been much different from that of any other prophet or civil rights worker. It is God's vindication in the resurrection that teaches us Jesus' universal meaning for salvation.

That is why we pray at Easter: "God, by raising Christ Your Son You conquered the power of death and opened for us the way to eternal life" (Opening Prayer). Be appreciative!

136

NLESS I see the print of the nails in His hands . . . I [Thomas] will not believe. — Jn 20:25

SEPT. 14

A Living Faith

Like love, faith is a gift of God, but we have reasons for it. We share our awareness of the Lord as fully alive with the early Church's experience as reported by witnesses. Along with the facts subtly theological commentary about the resurrection is also offered.

Study is mandatory as well as prayer with Thomas, "My Lord and my God!" (Jn 20:28). "Increase my faith! Let it be an ever more living reality in me especially when I need You."

 OME away by yourselves to a quiet place and rest a while. —Mk 6:31

SEPT. 15

Periodic Spiritual Renewal

On disembarking, the Lord Jesus and His disciples found the dearly needed "quiet place" already filled with a vast crowd. "Moved with pity," He did the most loving thing and began to teach them (Mk 6:34).

Busy as you are, do you feel the need for a "quiet place"? You have your car serviced regularly. You need a physical check-up every so often. What programs in the field of spiritual renewal are available in your parish? Do you take time for meditation? Married people who don't have time for one another will break up!

137

HY do Your disciples not live according to the tradition of the elders but instead eat a meal with hands defiled? —Mk 7:5

Renewal of Vatican II

Jesus answers the above question by saying, "You set aside God's commandment but cling to human tradition" (Mk 7:8). All religion, as organized by humans, needs a renewal or "clean-up" every so often. The Second Vatican Council has started it in our time.

Have you informed yourself? And if progressive, are you patient with those who have not kept up as yet? Bear with one another and pray for the Church, of which you are part.

F anyone wishes to be first, he must be last of all and servant of all.
— Mk 9:35

Real Greatness

These words of Jesus are clear but hard to carry out. After we have done a good job, even one of "service," we appreciate a pat on the shoulders. But how do you feel if you don't get it? It requires real greatness to go on serving without being appreciated by anyone except your heavenly Father.

You could look to Mary as an example. The Mighty One had done great things to her, yet she remained with Elizabeth for three months just "serving" (Lk 1:49, 56). Pray for real greatness.

BLESSED is the King Who comes in the name of the Lord.

— Lk 19:33

SEPT.

18

Christ the King

Jesus is King in the name of the Lord, but His kingdom "does not belong to this world" (Jn 18:36). Hence, we rightly believe in separation of Church and State. Does this mean, though, that Christian principles may not have an impact on our legislature? Let us enjoy our freedoms and be tolerant of others as long as they don't threaten our constitutional rights.

A Christian life-style and responsible voting habits are still the best proclamation of Jesus' kingship. "Thy kingdom come!"

JESUS cried out with a loud voice, "Father, into Your hands I commend My spirit."

— Lk 23:46

SEPT.

19

Look to the God-Man

Concerning the last moments of Jesus, Matthew and Mark describe Jesus as very restless: "My God, My God, why have You abandoned Me?" (Mt 27:26; Mk 15:34). Luke shows Him in prayer (Lk 23:46). John, who describes Jesus as fully aware of His divinity more than the synoptics do, has Jesus quietly bow His head and die (Jn 19:30). They thus show the human and divine sides of Jesus.

When down in the dumps, you should turn to the human and divine Jesus for guidance and strength.

139

ANY Samaritans . . . began to believe in Him [Jesus as the Messiah] because of the testimony of the woman. — Jn 4:39

Sharing the Faith

By courageously sharing her faith experience, the Samaritan woman was instrumental in converting her acquaintances. Do you show a similar courage? Note also that the Samaritans *began* to believe because of the woman who testified. Faith is a gift of God. That's why our testimony by both word and example must be accompanied by prayer.

Do you try every so often? Does your church sponsor an Inquiry Class to which you can refer "searchers"?

ET the one who is without sin among you be the first to cast a stone at her. — Jn 8:7

Love the Sinner

The scribes said to Jesus, "Moses commanded us to stone such women [adulteresses]" (Jn 8:5). Jesus answered with the above words. And those churchmen went away one by one (Jn 8:8-9). Condemning adultery and not condemning the adulteress can go hand in hand. Jesus did not condemn the woman.

Aware of our own sinfulness, we must be charitable in both thought and utterance. So often knowing all the circumstances means being understanding and forgiving.

F I, therefore, your Lord and Teacher, have washed your feet, you also ought to wash one another's feet. — Jn 13:14

SEPT.
22

Signs of Love

Love is the precious value most dealt with in poetry, music, plastic art, and symbolism. We have the washing of the feet, carried out by the Lord Jesus "before the feast of the Passover" and repeated in our Liturgy of Holy Thursday.

All of it makes sense only if it stands for genuine love, characterized by fidelity and real presence when needed. What about your "I love you," whenever and however uttered? "Lord, teach me to love!"

 EHOLD, I stand at the door and knock. — Rev 3:20

SEPT.
23

Freedom To Love

By creating us with a free will, in a sense God makes Himself defenseless. He wants us to respond freely to His invitation to live up to what we are designed to be. When I say "no" or answer only with a lukewarm "yes," God doesn't force me. He stands at the door and knocks. "If anyone hears My voice and opens the door [only then] I will come in" (Rev 3:20).

Love must motivate me to open up. Does it when I hear a poor fellow wayfarer ringing my doorbell or a coworker asks me for a favor? "God, increase my love!"

ND they were all filled with the Holy Spirit and began to speak in different tongues as the Spirit gave them utterance. — Act 2:4

Unity in Diversity

Thanks to the Spirit, devout Jews from every nation all heard the apostles speak in their own tongues (Act 2:5-13). In each of our congregations there is diversity in unity. There are "old timers," conservatives, and progressives.

Patiently, let us listen to that one language of love—the Spirit! "Scoffing," as narrowminded sectarians used to do, results in alienation and hatred (see Act 2:12). Only love makes us understand one another. Do you try?

HEY devoted themselves to the teaching of the apostles and the communal life, to the breaking of bread and prayers. — Act 2:42

Meaningful Worship

The description of that first congregation in Jerusalem contains a lesson for Christians of all times and cultures. We need one another's support. Don't ask what the Church can do for you on Sunday morning; ask what you can contribute to more meaningful worship, be it by just faithfully participating!

Are you involved in Church activity? "I will declare Your name to my brethren; *in the midst of the assembly* I will praise You" (Ps 22:23).

OW the company of believers was one in heart and mind, and none claimed any of his [or her] possessions as his [or her] own. — Act 4:32

Sharing Our Possessions

Luke adds, "There was not a needy person among them" (Act 4:34). In our huge parishes, we establish sodalities, prayer groups, and confraternities, which enable us to "feel at home" with those we know personally and with whom we can be united.

Are you a member of any parish group? "Sharing everything" requires a religious vocation, but there should be no needy! Do you visit a needy, aged, lonely parishioner every so often? Pray to the Holy Spirit, "Create a *new* heart in me!"

OR if this plan or this undertaking [the Christian movement] is of human origin, it will fail. — Act 5:38

The Gift of Discernment

Jewish leaders planned to nip the early Christian movement in the bud. But in the courtroom Gamaliel, a teacher of the Law, made the above statement, adding, "If it is of God, you will not be able to overthrow it" (Act 5:39).

Whether it concerns other human beings or situations in the Church (progressives versus conservatives), look at both sides before you judge. And in doubt let love be your guide! "Discernment of spirits" is a gift we must pray for.

ND hope does not disappoint us, because the love of God has been poured out into our hearts through the Holy Spirit Who has been given us. — Rom 5:5

Christian Hope

When the doctor shakes his head and says, "We have done everything possible," we know there is no hope any more. How do we as Christians handle hopeless situations? Hope is a virtue that goes with faith and love. It is a gift of God for which we must pray. Migraine, stress, depression, and even despair will be hovering over us as long as we are on our pilgrim way.

We can handle hopelessness if we believe that God wants the best for us even when we don't understand how (see Rom 5:5).

UT you are not in the flesh but in the spirit, if the Spirit of God dwells in you. — Rom 8:9

Living in the Spirit of God

In a crowded bus, people are not present to me as persons. I don't know them. We don't communicate. God is all-present, but His Spirit "dwells" [is at home] in us only if we communicate, i.e., if we open up to Him. We can then be "in the spirit," i.e., living not by the values of the flesh (our old self) but by those of our "born again" (from water and Spirit) selves.

I must constantly improve my communication, which consists in both speaking and listening. "Lord, teach me how to pray!"

YOU did not receive a spirit that makes you a slave again to fear.

—Rom 8:15

Love Rather Than Fear

In a well-balanced family, love rather than fear of punishment regulates daily life together. Hence, we should not look upon the Church mainly as an institution in which one observes a number of do's and don'ts in order to save one's soul. Fear of hell becomes the main motivation not to be disobedient.

Paul tells us that this should not be the case. We are God's children: "You received a Spirit of adoption, and by Him we cry, '*Abba*, Father'" (Rom 8:15). Check your motivations!

WELCOME anyone who is weak in the faith, without passing judgment on disputable matters.

—Rom 14:1

Instrument of God's Peace

In Paul's case, the problem was with Christians from Jewish background who still wanted to observe certain Jewish laws (festivals, dietary rules) and those who did not. Paul advocates giving and taking. Why do you judge others and look down on them? (Rom 14:10).

Can I accept a coworker or coparishioner as different? Even though I can silence him or her, can I leave it that way for the sake of peace? "Lord, make me an instrument of Your peace." Such an attitude is feasible in church work and certainly in the family.

HATEVER was written . . . was written to teach us, so that . . . we might have hope. — Rom 15:4

OCT.
2

Hope through God's Word

Paul refers to the Hebrew Scriptures, which we call the Old Testament. Like all literature, the Bible is conditioned by time and culture and needs to be explained by experts in the field. That's why we read Catholic editions of the Bible, with introductions and notes approved by the Church as reliable.

Think of the story of Job. What do you remember as written for your instruction and giving you hope? Grateful for God's word in the Bible, answer prayerfully.

EITHER the one who plants nor the one who waters is anything, but only God Who makes things grow.
—1 Cor 3:7

OCT.
3

Right Attitude toward Our Priests

Paul is offering a defense of priests and ministers. Not all are equally qualified, wise, amiable, eloquent in the pulpit or musical in the sanctuary. How long does it take you to "accept" a new pastor? Why should liking or disliking him not influence your allegiance to the Church or fidelity to your Church work?

Try to see priests as "servants of Christ and stewards of the mysteries of God"—who are to be trustworthy but are human as well (1 Cor 4:1-2). Pray for your pastor every so often.

UT now you have had yourself . . . justified in the name of the Lord Jesus Christ and by the Spirit of our God. — 1 Cor 6:11

Living as Christians

Paul first mentions what some of his converts in the port town of Corinth "used to be" (1 Cor 6:9-11). Let bygones be bygones. What counts is what you are now and must constantly try to be. Living as Christians is not easy. We must keep trying, though, and not judge others who fail in our eyes.

Don't forget your Christian dignity and have the courage to be different in both word and behavior if required. "Where there is darkness, let me sow light" (St. Francis).

 VERY athlete exercises self-control in every way.

— 1 Cor 9:25

Spiritual Exercises

Paul compares life to a race. Don't run "aimlessly," he says; "run to win" (1 Cor 9:26, 24). Seemingly, many people just sit down to eat and drink and rise up to revel (1 Cor 10:7). That's their way of living.

What are your goals in life? In order to achieve something you must "exercise self-control." It may be that "exercises" were overdone in the past. Now "sweet love" has replaced them! We need both! Lenten sacrifices still make sense. Doing the "most loving thing" is not always easy. You must keep training.

147

S OMEONE may say, "How are the dead raised? With what kind of body will they come back?" — 1 Cor 15:35

OCT.
6

Personal Resurrection

Paul reasons from a dichotomy of soul and body (1 Cor 15:36-49). Contemporary thinking does not speak of humans as "having" a body. I am my body! At death, the molecules that serve me return to where they came from. I, the person I made of myself during my lifetime, will live forever with God, in Whom I live now already, move, and have my being (Act 17:28).

Grateful and with God's help, keep growing into the lovable person you want to be for all eternity.

———————

E ACH one must test his own work . . . for each will have to bear his own load. — Gal 6:4-5

OCT.
7

Christian Caring

Paul states also, "Bear one another's burdens" (Gal 6:2). Caring for one another without getting meddlesome, protective, possessive, and judgmental requires unselfish love. "Minding your own business" and nevertheless "being concerned" is a kind of Christian rope dancing that we must practice daily. In this connection, Paul mentions examining your own work and not boasting (Gal 6:4).

Living together in a family or religious community without getting on one another's nerves presupposes "giving and taking" all the time. Pray for community virtues.

B E renewed in the spirit of your minds.
— Eph 4:23

OCT. 8

Means of Constant Renewal

Quite a few Christians become stale already at an early age. They have a closed mind. Retreats and missions are the traditional means of renewal. Keeping up with the right literature may be another. Reading the Bible with introductions and footnotes is very beneficial if it is done prayerfully.

Don't get old before your time, "darkened in understanding, separated from the life of God because of ignorance" (Eph 4:18). "Come, Holy Spirit, and enkindle in me the fire of Your love."

R ATHER, He emptied himself, taking the form of a servant.
— Phil 2:7

OCT. 9

Humility

Those who need status symbols and constant talk about their own achievements must look to the Master. Though He was in the form of God, He humbled Himself becoming obedient to death (Phil 2:6, 8). What makes me a somebody? If I value "having" over "being," I am on the wrong track. Jesus had nowhere to rest His head (Lk 9:58), but God exalted Him (Phil 2:9).

Check your conversations. Are they dealing too much with self and not listening enough? "God, help me to grow into the image of my Master!"

H E has rescued us from the power of darkness and brought us into to the kingdom of His beloved Son.

— Col 1:13

Our Need for Deliverance

Dark and dreary days make me moody. They should not, but they do. The moral darkness of ignorance, uncertainty, and guilt making one "moody" could be beneficial and make us appreciate God's gracious intervention in the human condition.

Do I feel the need for "deliverance" and being transferred to the "kingdom" of the Lord Jesus? Do I strive to "experience" it by prayerful surrender in love? It takes quiet, patience, and unconditional exposure. Try with God's help.

———————

L ET the peace of Christ rule in your hearts, for into that peace you were also called in the one body. — Col 3:15

The Peace of Christ

In order to achieve peace, Buddhist monks go through lengthy meditations and stern practices of self-denial. We share this ancient wisdom, but we qualify "peace" with "of Christ," as the author of Colossians does.

By meditation we create a vacuum, a situation of "detachment," as Orientals do, but we fill it with the Christian value of love. The more God, Who is love, dwells in us the more the peace of Christ rules our hearts and makes us happy. "Come, Spirit of God, fill the hearts of Your faithful."

EACH and admonish one another in all wisdom, singing psalms, hymns, and spiritual songs with gratitude in your hearts to God. — Col 3:16

Pray and Sing

Whether we sing "Happy Birthday" when Dad is 70 or the National Anthem on the Fourth of July, celebrations are inspiring. Equally inspiring should be the celebrations of our Christian mysteries. For too long we Catholics have been passive during the celebrations and the singing in our churches. Only now are we joining in more and singing more.

Actively and regularly participate in worship! We need one another's inspiration. "The person who sings well prays twice!"

OR from you the word of the Lord rang out . . . in every place.

— 1 Thes 1:8

Echoing God's Word

The word of the Lord should echo forth from us. But only when that word is conceived as Gospel, i.e., good news giving direction, happiness, and peace, can it sound with inspiration.

At the funeral of an old priest, the eulogizer said, "No priest of this diocese ever came to see him without finding a solution for his problems." Many came! Serenity and peace, God's word, sounded forth from him whenever I dropped by. What about you in your surroundings?

D O not quench the Spirit. Do not despise prophesying.

— 1 Thes 5:19

Accepting Others

We often pray that God's Spirit may enkindle in us the fire of His love. As in Paul's time, we have charismatics in our Church and members who foster the devotional. Do not despise them (1 Thes 5:20).

In our multicultural Church, I must be open-minded and not consider myself better than those who are more emotional than I may be. "Lord, help me to accept and even love people who are different from me."

———————

I F a man cannot know how to manage his own family, how can he take care of the church of God? — 1 Tim 3:5

Responsible Stewardship

Paul addresses Timothy, a married bishop. "He must manage his own family well, keeping his children under control with perfect dignity" (1 Tim 3:4). Responsible stewardship should be practiced by all. Married or single, we are not owners but stewards who must give account to our Maker. If we are not ready to do so, we may be exposed and shamed more than anyone shown on the TV screen when forced out of office because of corruption.

What about the penitential service every Sunday morning before Mass? Do you make it meaningful for *you*?

TOP drinking only water, but use a little wine for your stomach's sake.

— 1 Tim 5:23

OCT. **16**

Proper Use of Self-denial

Paul is concerned about Timothy, a young bishop, and tells him not to be so ascetic that he even avoids wine, the customary table drink in Southern Europe. For centuries, the Church has given us detailed rules of fast and abstinence. Now we realize that those rules were not goals in themselves but means to achieve detachment, which should free us for greater love.

Self-denial makes sense, for example, if it helps the poor (Operation "Rice Bowl"). Check, act, and pray!

OD did not give us a spirit of cowardice but rather a spirit of power and love and self-control.

—2 Tim 1:7

OCT. **17**

Ruling with Power and Love

In our context "power" does not mean "bossism" but "dynamic and energetic courage." The first interpretation represents the abuse of power, the second is a virtue, especially when exercised with love and self-control.

Wherever we are in charge, are our decisions made with great respect and love for others? As parents, do you lovingly reason with your teenagers but guide them with "power" as well? Pray for this "spirit" mentioned in the Second Letter to Timothy.

YOU know that everyone in Asia has deserted me. . . . May it not be held against them. —2 Tim 1:15; 4:16

The Remedy for Loneliness

Loneliness is a hardship with which all of us have to deal sooner or later. It is painful especially when caused by the default of those who supposedly are our friends. This happened to our Lord: "All the disciples deserted Him and fled" (Mt 26:56), and to Paul as shown in the Scripture quote above.

The best thing to do in such a case is to turn to the Lord, Who stood by Paul and gave him strength (2 Tim 4:17). "God, help me to grow in awareness of Your loving presence in me."

BE all the more zealous to make your call and election firm, for, in doing so, you will never fall. — 2 Pet 1:10

Fidelity to Our Call

We must supplement faith with virtue, virtue with knowledge, knowledge with self-control, self-control with endurance, endurance with devotion, devotion with mutual affection, and mutual affection with love (2 Pet 1:5—7). Mutual affection and love indicate togetherness as important for perseverance.

Are you actively involved in Liturgy and Church work, where you encounter others on a person-to-person basis? Pray for growth in affection and love, which makes your "call" firm!

WHOEVER claims to be in the light but hates his brother is still in the darkness. —1 Jn 2:9

Forgiving Others

God is light (1 Jn 2:5). As baptized Christians, we are in God and God is in us. And having fellowship with God means having fellowship with one another. There is no room for hatred.

Think of a person who hurt your feelings recently. How did you handle it? Considering his or her background and saying a prayer for him or her helps to forgive and forget. Follow your Master, Who prayed on the cross, "Father, forgive them, for they do not know what they are doing" (Lk 23:34).

THE world and its enticements are passing away. But whoever does the will of God lives forever. — 1 Jn 2:17

Time and Eternity

About to celebrate his golden anniversary in the priesthood, a friend of mine wrote, "It has gone so fast!" You don't need faith to agree with him. It goes fast.

The second part of the above Bible quote requires faith. I think of Sts. Agatha, Lucy, and Cecilia, young women who died as martyrs centuries ago. The Church still remembers them in Eucharistic Prayer I. "Lord, give me some of the faith of these martyrs to always see life in its right perspective."

ET what you have heard from the beginning abide in you. . . . Then you will abide in the Son and in the Father.

— 1 Jn 2:24

First Faith

I was no older than four and at home alone with my mother when she received word that her mother had died. She cried, knelt down at the dining room table, and prayed the rosary. Crying softly, I recited the Hail Mary's with her. I still keep my mother's rosary in the glove compartment of my car.

Do you have a similar disclosure experience connected with the beginning? Do you gratefully remember it? To me, the memory of my mother praying the rosary is still inspiring.

 EE what love the Father has lavished on us, that we should be called children of God. —1 Jn 3:1

Children of God

Numerous homeless children roam the streets of any big city. They lack any awareness of belonging. I know how difficult it is to sell the values of love and belonging to children who have never experienced them. The exact details of how we shall be God's children later have not been revealed (1 Jn 3:2). But I can surmise them based on my happy childhood at home.

Be grateful if yours was a pleasant one and take it as a basis to meditate on your childhood in God and grow in appreciation.

OD is love, and whoever abides in love abides in God and God abides in him.
— 1 Jn 4:16

The Mystery of God

The mystery of God cannot be explained in feeble human language. The Bible speaks of God as king, judge, army commander, and creator. Two clear highlights are Christ's designation of God as Father and John's designation of Him as Love. God loved us first; so we are able to love (1 Jn 4:19).

Keep your relationship of love alive. There is no fear in love (see 1 Jn 4:18). We can outgrow fear the more we respond in generous love, kept growing by communication, which is called "meditative prayer."

 OU have abandoned the love you had at first. . . . Repent, and do the works you did at first.
— Rev 2:4-5

Keeping Love for God Vital

The Church of Ephesus had abandoned its first love. This is a sign of upcoming alienation between us and God our spouse (Isa 54:5), and it often ends up in separation. How come? God does not make mistakes. Could it be that too many of us see our relationship with God mainly as a legal rather than a loving one?

What do you do to foster love, affection, and intimacy with God, in Whom you live and move and have your being? God is love! (see Act 17:28; 1 Jn 4:16).

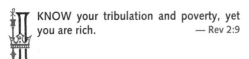

KNOW your tribulation and poverty, yet you are rich. — Rev 2:9

Overcoming Every Tribulation

"Tribulation" comes in many guises: chemical dependency of a spouse or child, a stale marital or vowed life situation, a financial crisis, or a child who dropped out of school.

The author of Revelation tells the Church of Smyrna, "Do not be afraid of what you are about to suffer" (Rev 2:10). He even states, "You are rich." Does this sound crazy? Yet, "be faithful until death, and I [God] will bestow on you the crown of life" (Rev 2:10).

HESE are the words of the Amen: "I wish you were either cold or hot." — Rev 3:15

The Danger of Indifference

Soup must be served hot and beer cold. A temperature in between makes them nauseating. Applied to the realm of interpersonal relationship, the metaphor is clear. God tells the Church of Laodicea, "Because you are lukewarm—neither hot nor cold—I will spew you out of My mouth" (Rev 3:16). Indifference kills love. A young woman asks her lover every so often, "Did you think of me?"

How do you relate to God? Do you really need Him and think of Him? He loves you. He stands at the door and knocks (Rev 3:20). "So be earnest and repent" (Rev 3:19).

H E [Jesus] asked them, "Who do you say I am?" — Mt 16:15

Son of the Living God

Jesus is a fascinating figure. But who is He—just another slain prophet like John the Baptist? In the New Testament we observe a growing awareness that Jesus is the cause of definitive salvation for all people of all times. Peter says, "You are the Christ, the Son of the living God" (Mt 16:16).

In faith we share this inspired awareness and confess it whenever we conclude our official prayers with "We ask this . . . through Jesus Christ, Your Son our Lord."

———————

W HAT kind of Man is this? Even the winds and the sea obey Him? — Mt 8:27

God's Power in Jesus

Jesus "rebuked the winds and the sea, and there was complete calm" (Mt 8:26). Rather than searching for what has really happened in any of the miracle narratives, we seek to understand how the early Church recognizes in those events the presence of God. "Save us, Lord! We are perishing!" (Mt 8:25).

Matthew teaches that God's power resides in Jesus. Regardless of how violent the upheavals in our lives may be, the Lord can save us if we but turn to Him in faith. "What kind of Man is this?" "Lord, increase my little faith!"

MAN named Zacchaeus, . . . a chief tax collector and rich, was seeking to see who Jesus was. — Lk 19:2-3

OCT. 30

Desire To Know Jesus

Though in the category of "loanshark" in our culture, Zacchaeus was inquisitive, which is the beginning of wisdom and can lead to salvation. Many are not inquisitive except for the football scores or the latest soap opera affair.

The tax collector's search for Jesus' identity was rewarded with "salvation" (Lk 19:9). Our Lord has given direction to millions of people. Don't you want to know more about Him? What about your *meditative* search for Him in the Bible?

 HEN it was evening, at sunset . . . the whole town was gathered together by the door. — Mk 1:32-33

OCT. 31

A Charismatic Preacher

What sort of Man is Jesus? We learn about Him from His ministry: exorcism, healing, miracles, all related to His teaching about the Kingdom of God (see Mk 1:21-45). Jesus was a charismatic preacher more in line with the prophets of Israel than with the scribes, i.e., the administrators. Religion needs institution—but as a means not as a goal in itself!

Are you fascinated by Christ and what He stands for—living your dedication, though, in the framework of your Church?

OR the marriage of the Lamb has come, and His bride has made herself ready.

— Rev 19:7

The Victory of the Lamb

We are invited to celebrate the marriage of the Messiah with the Church, His bride. "The Lord has established His reign" (Rev 19:6). His is final victory over evil. The whole tenet of the Book of Revelation is the assertion to Christians that final victory will be theirs at the wedding of Christ with His people.

"Let us rejoice and be glad" (Rev 19:7) and be sure to be "in that number!" "Let me not be put to shame, O Lord, for I cry out to You. . . . Save me in Your kindness" (Ps 31:18, 17).

E [Christ] also went to preach to the spirits in prison, who had long ago been disobedient . . . [that] they might live in the spirit.

—1 Pet 3:19-20; 4:6

Purification for the Dead

The author teaches a judgment of purification for the dead, after salvation was announced to them by Jesus. His death has universal value, and because of it all the just who suffer can do so for others. The Second Book of Maccabees teaches the same thing.

We do not know how God responds to prayer in a situation in which there is no time and space. We follow our tradition and pray, "Welcome into Your kingdom our departed brothers and sisters" (Eucharistic Prayer III).

THE book of the genealogy of Jesus Christ, the son of David, the son of Abraham — Mt 1:1

Jesus, the Anointed One

"Christ" means "Anointed One." Oil is a symbol of strength. "The men of Judah came and anointed David king of the Judahites" (2 Sam 2:4). Once enthroned, the king was seen as God's representative to the people. The New Testament writers describe Jesus as such a king, descendant of their legendary king David.

And as "Christ" He claims dominion over all creation, also over you (see Preface of Christ the King). Do you see Him as your leader, the One Who gives direction to your life?

———

JESUS answered [Pilate], "My kingdom does not belong to this world." — Jn 18:36

Extending God's Kingdom

Jesus reigns over God's kingdom, initiated in the hearts of all persons of goodwill and to be fully realized in the hereafter. Gentle persuasion must establish that kingdom, not force. If not, said Jesus, "My servants would be fighting" (Jn 18:36). Unfortunately, the various Churches have not always realized this!

We should respect Christians who do not think and worship exactly as we do. Your kindness, understanding, and good example are the ways to extend God's kingdom around us. "Thy kingdom come."

N Antioch the disciples were called Christians for the first time.

— Act 11:26

NOV.

5

Christians—Followers of Christ

For a while the Christian movement was known as "The Way" (Act 24:22). Soon Christ's followers were called "Christians." It is our most apt name up till now, since it brings out clearly our dedication to Christ and what He stands for.

Are you a Christian your Church can be proud of? Word, example, and loyalty should show it. "Lord, help me to stand for what I claim to be."

———————

AUL [demonstrated] that . . . "This is Jesus, Whom I proclaim to you is the Messiah."

— Act 17:2-3

NOV.

6

Jesus the Messiah

The title "Messiah" is the most frequently used one to designate Who the risen Jesus is. Unfortunately, it was overloaded with political connotations. However, Jesus wanted to be the Messiah Who delivered humankind not from political servitude but from the servitude of sin (see Mt 4:1-11). God's kingdom had to be established by persuasion not coercion (see Jn 18:36).

In our very human Church, you and I should extend God's kingdom by gentle persuasion! Is your life-style inspiring both unbelievers and other Christians?

163

GOD in this way brought to fulfillment
. . . that His Messiah would suffer.

— Act 3:18

A Suffering Messiah

Like all suffering, Jesus' suffering remains a mystery even for believers. In faith we can approach it, but there is no adequate explanation. Can a leader who dies in pain and humiliation be salvific?

If you are suffering and looking for direction, you may learn how to handle your pain by meditating on our Lord's passion. Groping in darkness, He prayed: "Remove this cup from Me, yet not what I will but what You will" (Mk 14:36).

THUS we shall always be with the Lord.

— 1 Thes 4:17

Perfect and Lasting Bliss

In Tchaikovsky's "Nutcracker," Clara is carried off to a magic kingdom, where acrobats and dancers entertain her and her prince—for one night only! Seeking perfect and lasting bliss on earth is foolish. Our yearning will be satisfied when the kingdom reaches completion in the hereafter: "What God has prepared for those who love Him" (1 Cor 2:9).

This knowledge made Paul state, "I desire to depart this life and be with Christ" (Phil 1:23). He knew Him in a person-to-person relationship! "Lord, increase my faith."

E will rule over the house of Jacob forever, and of His kingdom there will be no end. — Lk 1:33

Growing in Knowledge of Jesus

The early Church experienced Jesus in His exaltation as "Messiah," anointed with a Holy Spirit and power (see Act 10:38). The faithful also came to understand that Jesus was already "Messiah" during His earthly ministry and consequently from the very moment of His incarnation, and gradually the understanding developed that He is a divine Messiah.

Does your awareness of Who Jesus is grow constantly? Prayerful Bible reading is mandatory for this growth in awareness.

HE God of our ancestors has glorified His servant Jesus, Whom you delivered up and denied in the presence of Pilate. — Act 3:13

Greatness of the Servant

The New Testament writers turned to the Hebrew Bible for paradigms to describe Who Jesus was. Identifying Jesus with the suffering servant of God in Isaiah (chapters 42, 49, 50, 52), they support their inspired claim that His suffering was salvific for all of us: "Christ died for our sins in accordance with the Scriptures" (1 Cor 15:3). A servant can be great!

Can God glorify you for being "a servant," humbly regarding others as more important than yourself? (see Phil 2:3).

165

ETER answered Him, . . . "We believe and are convinced that You are the Holy One of God." — Jn 6:68-69

NOV.
11

Sharing God's Holiness

At one point, Peter tells the people, "You disowned the Holy and Righteous One and asked for a murderer to be released to you" (Act 3:14). The attribute "holy" is usually applied to God, Who alone is holy, sinless, and absolutely perfect. Peter calls Jesus holy. Rejected by His own, Jesus did not open His mouth.

Sharing God's holiness may imply rejection by those whose values are not Christian. "God, give me the courage to be a Christian," i.e., dedicated to "the Holy One of God."

HEN [Ananias] said, "The God of our ancestors appointed you . . . to see the Righteous One." — Act 22:14

NOV.
12

Concentrate on Jesus

Paul had "seen" Jesus, the Righteous One, in a disclosure experience, which was decisive for the rest of his life (see Act 9:19). Untiringly traveling from town to town, he became the witness of this righteous and godly Man from Nazareth.

When making ethical decisions, don't check first the law on the books. It may result in a calculating minimalism. Look to Jesus, the Righteous One! Hear the sound of His voice in Scripture. He is the inspiring challenge to real greatness.

166

OU put to death the Author [Leader, Pioneer] of life, but God raised Him from the dead. — Act 3:15

NOV. 13

Improving Our Lives

Salvation in and through Jesus is related to life, a good life, mainly seen as relational now and hereafter. The quality of our relationships makes life human. That is what the Bible thinks of when it calls Jesus the "Author of life." By raising Jesus from the dead God has vindicated His efforts to improve life as related to both other human beings and Almighty God.

Where does your life need improvement? For direction, look to the Author of life!"

 ET us run the race . . . while fixing our eyes on Jesus, the Leader and Perfecter of our faith. — Heb 12:1-2

NOV. 14

Jesus Our Coach

The author of Hebrews pictures life as an athletic contest and Jesus as the coach; Christians in the ring fighting their opponent sin; and "a cloud of witnesses" cheering them on. We must "rid ourselves of all that hinders and sin that clings to us" and persevere (Heb 12:1).

The author uses images from the Roman amphitheater to tell us what life is all about and where Jesus fits in. Being in the race or boxing contest, you must have faith in your coach. Hence, keep your eyes fixed on Jesus. From your prayerful Bible reading, what is your mental picture of Jesus?

167

OSES said: "The Lord, your God, will raise up for you a prophet like me." — Act 3:22

Jesus the Prophet

Luke, the author of the Acts of the Apostles, quotes Deuteronomy 18:15 and applies Moses' words to Jesus, Whom he describes as another Moses, actually as more than Moses. Jesus is *the* prophet, the One Who is to come into the world (see Jn 6:14). He is God's definitive spokesperson to you and me.

Are you accepting Jesus as Luke sees Him whenever you encounter Him in your Bible? "God, open my eyes and ears for what You have to tell me in and through Jesus. Increase my faith!"

T this the bearers stood still. And He said, "Young man, I say to you, arise." —Lk 7:14

Another Elijah

Elijah was a fiery prophet, taken up in a whirlwind (see 1 Ki 17—19; Sir 48:1-4; 2 Ki 2). In Jesus' time, people expected Elijah to return. Some saw him in John the Baptist. Luke describes Jesus as an Elijah-like prophet, raising a young man from the dead. (Compare Lk 7:11-17 and 1 Ki 17:17-24.)

Jesus is God's spokesperson, a great prophet, endowed with the life-giving power that we need if we are to keep moving. When sluggish, arise! Listen to Jesus and pray for inspiration.

ESUS is "the stone that was rejected by you, the builders, but has become the cornerstone."
—Act 4:11

NOV.
17

Jesus the Cornerstone

In Israel stones were used to build houses. The cornerstone kept two walls together. And that's what Jesus' function is. He keeps families, congregations, and friends together. Hatred, jealousy, and selfishness are the divisive forces that reject Him. Love, which He preaches, is the cement that unites.

Wherever there is danger of splitting up, turn to the Lord Jesus, and by all means let your presence be a uniting one. "Where there is hatred, let me sow love" (St. Francis).

HE Son of Man will be handed over to men, and they will kill Him; then after three days He will rise.
— Mk 9:31

NOV.
18

Redemptive Suffering

Approaching the mystery of Christ and His redemptive work, the Gospels depict Jesus as another suffering servant of Yahweh as found in Isaiah (chs 49, 50, 52, and 53). His disciples at first did not understand.

As His disciple, do I accept the Lord Jesus as a servant and suffering as redemptive? I am not autonomous, and pain as part and parcel of life must be redemptive somehow. Pray for faith and a living hope in the resurrection (see Mk 8:38).

AN the guests of the Bridegroom fast while He is with them?
— Mk 2:19

Love for God in Jesus

The bridal metaphor brings out the intimate relationship God wants with us in Jesus. The disciples of John and of the Pharisees were accustomed to fast (see Mk 2:18). Jesus fasted and said that His followers would as well, "when the Bridegroom has been taken away" (Mk 2:20).

We should fast and do works of charity boosting our Christian identity by fostering the value of love for God, Who is our lover in Jesus. Do we? How?

_____

E said to them, "This is My blood of the Covenant, which is shed for many. "
—Mk 14:24

Surrendering Oneself in Love

The servant of the Lord in Isaiah (53:12) surrendered himself to death and took away the sins of many. Mark depicts the Lord Jesus as such a servant in His meritorious suffering.

And in memory of Him we reenact what He did (see Mk 14:23). We pray, "May we become one body, one spirit in Christ and be made an everlasting gift to You [God]" (Eucharistic Prayer III). With Christ, surrendering yourself in love frees you from your captivity of egotism, and as such it is redemptive. (See May 27.)

THIS is My beloved Son. With Him I am well pleased. Listen to Him.
— Mt 17:5

Beloved Son

Jesus is identified as the one to be listened to like God's spokespersons Moses and Elijah (see Ex 2—4; Deut 34; 1 Ki 17—19; and Sir 48:1-4). Steeped in the Hebrew Bible, the Gospel writers borrowed concepts to bring out Who Jesus is.

We can't always have a disclosure awareness like that of the disciples, who "fell on their faces and were very much afraid." Usually, we see, "no one else but Jesus only" (Mt 17:6-8). Do we accept Him as such, God's spokesperson to be listened to?

OR even the Son of Man did not come to be served but to serve and to give His life as a ransom for many.   — Mk 10:45

Vicarious Suffering

"Vicarious suffering" is part and parcel of Hebrew theology. By using it to explain the vicarious suffering of the Lord Jesus, New Testament authors may suggest that God is a cruel sadist Who enjoys the pain of victims.

In reality, we must see Jesus' suffering in the framework of His task as a whole: an exemplary life of surrender in love—with suffering as part of it. As such it is vicarious and redemptive. Are you ready to follow the Lord and be redeemed?

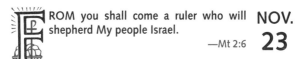

FROM you shall come a ruler who will shepherd My people Israel.

—Mt 2:6

How To Find Jesus

With his story on the Magi searching for the newborn King of the Jews by following His star, Matthew teaches how to see Jesus, namely, as a Ruler, a Shepherd, Who gives both direction and protection. And he shows how to find Him, by following the light of faith—as radiated especially in Scripture.

Like Herod's scribes, we should search the Scriptures in order to find Jesus: "Entering the house, they saw the Child with Mary His mother" (Mt 2:11). "Father, lead us to Your glory in heaven by the light of faith."

———————————

THE Son of Man has come eating and drinking; and you say, Behold . . . "a friend of tax collectors and sinners."

— Lk 7:34

Jesus: God-with-Us

Jesus called Himself "Son of Man," which can mean a human being, one of us. Yet the wisdom of God was incarnated in Him to such an extent that in later reflection He is simply called "God" with the understanding, though, that He remains "Man" as well. This is a mystery that goes beyond human understanding.

In faith we approach it and are grateful for God's closeness, His being "Emmanuel," with us is God (Mt 1:23). Spending time with Jesus means being with God, Whose image He is!

S this Man not the carpenter, the son of Mary, and the brother of James and Joses . . . ? — Mk 6:3

NOV. 25

Accepting Truth Where Found

Jesus, a local boy, taught in the synagogue at Nazareth. The people were astonished. "What kind of wisdom has been given Him?" Lack of faith made His neighbors reject Him (Mk 6:2-6).

Can I accept truth, direction, and even correction from regardless who forwards it? "Man's pride brings him low" (Prov 29:23). Exploring God's wisdom in whatever sort of clothing it comes to you requires faith and humility. Pray for both of these virtues!

———————

HERE two or three come together in My name, there am I in the midst of them. — Mt 18:20

NOV. 26

Remedy for Loneliness

Loneliness is a frightening phenomenon in the human condition. And happily married, single, or religious, all of us must finally go it alone. Faith, though, indicates a lasting element in all togetherness. We have our Lord's final promise: "I am with you always, until the close of the age" (Mt 28:20).

Being with others in church is meaningful and can be a remedy for loneliness—so long as your congregation is a real family of believers, aware of Christ in our midst. Pray for a growing awareness.

N OW, Master, You may dismiss Your servant in peace for my eyes have seen Your salvation. —Lk 2:29-30

Journeying in the Dark

"Salvation" implies rescue from the fright of a meaningless existence. "What is life for?" Is it just for eating, drinking, loving, quarreling, having fun, and enduring pain with a final transition into the nothingness where we came from? Journeying in the dark, without the light of faith, is frightening. Simeon in Lk 2:22-32 shows how one can grow old graciously. He came into the temple "in the spirit" and recognized Jesus.

Open your eyes and you will be saved from darkness and no sense of direction in life. Don't wait, though, till you are old!

AUL began at once to proclaim Jesus in the synagogues, saying, "He is the Son of God." — Act 9:20

Son of God

As "Son of God," i.e., His representative to the people, Jesus is a king endowed with absolute authority. He represents Almighty God by ruling, judging, and providing.

We must accept our Lord not only as "sweet Jesus" but also as the One Who authoritatively tells us how to fashion our lives and Who is entitled to enforce Divine Law as "judge of the living and the dead" (Nicene Creed). Let the Profession of Faith, which we say after the Sunday sermon, really be "yours!"

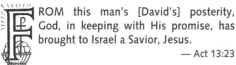

ROM this man's [David's] posterity, God, in keeping with His promise, has brought to Israel a Savior, Jesus.

— Act 13:23

Salvation in Jesus

Paul describes Jesus as a Savior in line with the great national heroes of Israel (Act 13:14-22). It is sad that the early preachers failed to convince the Jewish people as a whole that Jesus continues their salvation history—not politically but on a higher, spiritual and universal level. God's promise implies salvation both from slavery and for freedom.

How are you aware of "salvation from and for" in your situation? Pray for courage to continue the process!

———————

E [God] has given assurance to all people by raising [Jesus] from the dead.

— Act 17:31

Rooted in the Resurrection

In his speech at the Areopagus, Paul addresses highly educated pagan Athenians. Jesus' credibility stands and falls with His being vindicated in the resurrection, which can be known only in faith. Faith, an intuition, is a gift of God for which we have reasons, i.e., the testimony of the early Christians.

You have reasons why you love your spouse, though they may not be very convincing to others! Love and faith are akin. Keep alive both gifts by prayerfully loving and believing.

175

E [Paul] bore witness . . . to be repentant before God and to have faith in our Lord Jesus. — Act 20:21

Loving and Believing

Why could Scrooge, the miser in Dickens' *A Christmas Carol*, not celebrate Christmas? He was selfish; he had first to repent and to be converted to love. Only a loving person can be a believing person. Faith and love are intimately related. We should foster both with the same means. When harassed by doubts, young intellectuals so often overlook this point.

Do I handle faith the same way I handle love? How could Paul (who was no dummy) go on bearing witness? (see Act 20:22-24).

 OD is faithful, and by Him you were called into the fellowship of His Son, Jesus Christ our Lord. — 1 Cor 1:9

Fellowship with the Lord

"Jesus is Lord" is repeated often in Paul's writings, though we can say it only "by the Holy Spirit," i.e., in faith (see 1 Cor 12:3). Paul loved Jesus (Rom 8:35), but he strikes the balance. He is conscious of Christ's kingship (being Lord) as well.

Fellowship with Jesus is our precious prerogative. We may love Him as a friend, but we are also aware that His "gentle rule" is beneficial. Keep this relationship alive by prayerful dialogue and by union with the Lord in the Eucharist.

GIVE thanks to my God always for you because of the grace of God that was bestowed on you in Christ Jesus.

DEC. 3

—1 Cor 1:4

The Grace Bestowed on Us

Paul sees his congregation in a busy port town as "enriched in every way," while awaiting the revelation of our Lord Jesus Christ (1 Cor 1:5-7). Their daily lives of hard shoreline labor had not changed with Baptism, but they were enriched with the grace of God in Jesus, so that they could keep moving.

Whatever our task in life and the pressures we are under, are we aware and grateful? Would I be able to make it without faith-religion, or the grace God has given me in Jesus?

UST as in Adam all die, so also in Christ shall all be made alive.

DEC. 4

—1 Cor 15:22

Life in Christ

Paul depicts Adam as a literary type of Christ. In the story of Genesis, God blew into his nostrils the breath of life (Gen 2:7). The first man, Adam, became a living being, the last Adam (Christ) a life-giving spirit. As children of Adam, we bear his image and must die. As Christians, we shall bear the image of the heavenly Adam and live forever.

Accepting this in faith, we are grateful and console one another whenever one of our beloved ones departs "so that [we] may not grieve like other people, who have no hope" (1 Thes 4:13).

177

H E [Jesus] is the image of the invisible God.

— Col 1:15

Jesus Our Light

Paul states, "The god of this world has blinded the minds of unbelievers, so that they cannot see" (2 Cor 4:4). Which "god" (shows, literature, bad habits, friends) is blinding your eyes or even endangering your life as a Christian?

"In [Jesus] we see our God made visible and so are caught up in love of the God we cannot see" (Preface of Christmas). Meditation-contemplation should result in our being caught up in love and driving safely to our destination!

F OR those whom God foreknew He also predestined to be conformed to the image of His Son.

— Rom 8:29

The Family of Christ

The authors of the Bible, most of them Jewish, were very family oriented and use it often as a paradigm to depict what the Church ought to be: a family of believers, sisters and brothers under the universal fatherhood of God with Christ as the firstborn. "In love [God] destined us to be adopted as His sons through Jesus Christ" (Eph 1:5).

Do I fit into this family? I must be willing to be conformed ever more to the image of Christ. What virtue do you consider paramount in your family or religious community? How do you practice it in the framework of your parish?

HRIST has in fact been raised from the dead, the firstfruits of those who have fallen asleep.   —1 Cor 15:20

Christ the Firstfruits

In nursing homes, elderly people are encouraged to exercise together. We cannot live forever, but we want to keep ourselves in good shape as long as possible. We cherish life.

In Hebrew worship, a portion of the harvest, the firstfruits, was offered to God and in it the entire harvest. Paul sees the risen Christ as "firstfruits" and in Him all of us destined for life everlasting. Our yearning to live will be fulfilled! "God, I am grateful for the gift of life and of everlasting life."

LESSED are you among women, and blessed is the fruit of your womb.
                                    — Lk 1:42

Be Proud in the Lord!

This is Elizabeth's greeting to Mary. Indeed, Mary is blessed, but she does not brag. Luke describes Mary's response by putting a psalm into her mouth, "For He [God] has looked upon the lowliness of His handmaid" (Lk 1:48).

Being proud of what we have achieved in life is good as long as we see it in the perspective of our total dependence on God. "He Who is mighty has done great things for me" (Lk 1:49). Whenever we talk about ourselves we should proclaim the Lord's greatness (see Lk 1:46).

UE to [God] . . . you are in Christ Jesus, Who has become for us wisdom from God—i.e. . . . righteousness, sanctification, and redemption.   — 1 Cor 1:30

The Grace To Be a Christian

Who was doing a favor to whom when you accepted your call and now live as a Christian? "Boasting before God," pretending that you are able to make it by your own resources, is sinful (see 1 Cor 1:26-31).

Paul mentions what Christ means to you: wisdom from God, righteousness, sanctification, redemption. Reflect on the how, when, and where of each meaning and thank God! "Let whoever boasts, boast in the Lord" (1 Cor 1:31).

———

 HRIST Himself is our peace, Who has made both [Jews and Gentiles] one and broken the dividing wall of enmity, through His flesh. — Eph 2:14

No Happiness without Peace

We may see a dividing wall between those who accept and those who reject Christianity. As the "extended Christ," we should preach peace by word and example on the job and wherever we come in contact with unbelievers.

But we must also preach peace to those who are near and don't think exactly as we do (see Eph 2:14). Any dividing wall causes alienation. And without peace there is no happiness. Are you a peacemaker?

HERE is one Mediator between God and the human race, the Man Christ Jesus. — 1 Tim 2:5-6

DEC. 11

Christ Our Mediator

With the Jews, we Christians are aware of the awe-inspiring greatness of God. Hence, we repeatedly pray to Him through our Mediator, Jesus Christ. Being conscious of our own sinfulness, we know that there is One Who is human like us but sinless. "Through Him we both [Jews and Gentiles] have access to the Father by one Spirit" (Eph 2:18).

Think of this when you pray in church "We ask this through our Lord Jesus Christ, Your Son."

HE [Christ] is always able to save those who come to God through Him. — Heb 7:25

DEC. 12

Jesus Saves!

Though only God saves human beings, Jesus saves as well. His life of dedicated ministry, His suffering, death, and resurrection are the exemplary cause of our salvation. Secondly, Jesus' sacrifice on the cross was a form of prayer, which He continues in heaven (see Rom 8:34).

However, remember that with human concepts we are approaching an unfathomable mystery: God saves us! Be grateful and whenever you are in trouble approach God through our Lord Jesus Christ.

CHRIST is the head of the body, the Church.

— Col 1:18

The Body of Christ

We are "Christ's body, and each one [of us] is a part of it" (1 Cor 12:27). As all parts of the body have their own function, so do the members of the Church. We should work with one another but most of all with Christ, head of the body, the Church.

If there is friction, dissent, or dislike of those heading the institution, don't despair! Your final dedication is to Christ and what He stands for. Meditatively turn to Him, the head from which all insight, direction, and inspiration is forthcoming.

HOLY "brothers," who share a heavenly calling, reflect on Jesus, the apostle and high priest Whom we confess.

— Heb 3:1

Jesus the High Priest

Jesus is a high priest, entering into the sanctuary of heaven, though not with the blood of goats and calves but with His own blood, thus obtaining eternal redemption (Heb 9:12). He is a high priest Who can sympathize with our weaknesses, because He has been tested and tempted as we are daily (Heb 4:15). He is a high priest Who offered prayers and supplications with loud cries (at Gethsemane) and tears and was heard (Heb 5:7).

Reflect on Him and turn to Him in prayer.

FOR in Christ dwells the whole fullness of the deity in bodily form, and you share in this fullness. — Col 2:9-10

Jesus, True God and Eternal Life

The Christian awareness that the wisdom-word-light of God is so united with Jesus that He may be called God (1 Jn 5:20)—with the understanding that He remains Man as well—is a mystery. Analogously, we believe God to be a person, but we don't have an adequate concept of Him. Neither do we understand human personhood. Hence, the union of both is even more mysterious.

We bow our heads and are grateful that in Jesus God is Emmanuel and that somehow we may share in this fullness.

BEHOLD, the Lamb of God, Who takes away the sin of the world.

—Jn 1:29

The Expiating Lamb

Actively, Jesus had opposed evil and healed the wounds of sin and division. Passively, He took away the sin of the world by expiating it like a Jewish Passover lamb. Neither God nor Jesus wanted the cruel outcome of His life as a slain lamb. He accepted the inevitable (Mk 14:36). Armed with Jesus' "attitude" (1 Pet 4:1), we too should strike the balance between being active and passive in searching for a meaningful life.

After I have done all I can, do I try to accept the factual?

ORTHY is the Lamb, Who was slain, to receive power and riches, wisdom and strength, honor and glory and praise. — Rev 5:12

DEC. 17

The Victorious Lamb

Artists have competed with the author of Revelation in depicting the victory of the risen Christ, the Paschal Lamb, slain but vindicated by God in the resurrection. Think of Van Eyck's wonderful painting "The Adoration of the Lamb!"

We must identify with the Lamb, slain but finally victorious. Only by going the way of the cross can we celebrate Easter. "Lord, keep me steadfast in the Faith, when pain and frustration come my way. I need Your wisdom and strength!"

———————

N the beginning was the Word, and the Word was with God, and the Word was God. — Jn 1:1

DEC. 18

The Word of God

Christ as preexistent was "with God" and became incarnate. Life, light, truth, and testimony are the metaphors John uses to depict what "the Word made flesh" means to us.

God's light shines in the darkness of our human condition (Jn 1:5), but exposing yourself to it is mandatory in order to enjoy its benefits. Keep eyes and ears open in daily meditation, lest you end up with "His own" who did not accept Him (Jn 1:11).

MEN, amen, I say to you, before Abraham came to be, I AM.

— Jn 8:58

The Mystery of Being

Referring to God's self-identification to Moses from the burning bush (Ex 3:14), Jesus clearly brings out His own divinity. We humans came to be; God is!

"Being" remains a mystery. All I know is that I share being with God. Moreover, I have learned that "being" should take precedence over "having." Do I cultivate "being" by growing ever more into the likeness of the source of my being? It requires reflection, prayer, and contemplation!

———

[JESUS] am the Bread of Life.

— Jn 6:35

The Bread of Life

According to the media, the best bread must be "natural whole grain goodness" and "enriched" with vitamins and fibers! Jesus calls Himself "Bread" enriched with life as such! In our country of plenty, with its overflowing resources, most of us have never experienced hunger; hence, we must try to understand Jesus' metaphor, "Whoever eats this Bread will live forever" (Jn 6:51), especially when we receive Holy Communion.

Standing in the communion line, be aware that you need the Lord, His guidance and His strength, to keep moving. Avoid routine!

[JESUS] am the Light of the World. Whoever follows Me will . . . have the light of life.

— Jn 8:12

The Light of the World

Times Square and 42nd Street in New York and the Las Vegas Strip in Nevada seemingly don't know darkness. But where are those abundant neon lights directing the eager tourist? Can Jesus, Light of the World, compete?

Not losing your sense of direction requires maturity and faith. You have been meditating on Who Jesus of Nazareth is. Is it worthwhile to follow Him? Don't lose your sense of direction by making detours. Keep your "eyes fixed on Jesus" (Heb 12:2). In previous meditations, which titles of Jesus appeal most to you?

AM the Good Shepherd. The Good Shepherd lays down His life for the sheep.

— Jn 10:11

The Good Shepherd

We are not acquainted with sheepfolds, shepherds, and sheep. But reading the Bible, you often come across them, as used to teach religious values. Sometimes, TV has shows about this disappearing phenomenon of sheep and shepherds. "Whoever wants to understand the poet must enter the poet's land" (Goethe).

The point here is that the Lord Jesus cares and knows you personally. Do you know Him and consequently appreciate His care and loving presence?

ESUS said . . . , "I am the Way and the Truth and the Life. No one comes to the Father except through Me. — Jn 14:6

DEC.
23

Jesus the Way to the Father

Responding to Philip's request, "Master, show us the Father" (Jn 14:8), Jesus refers to "belief and love" (Jn 14:11, 15). Intellectuals (like Thomas the Doubter: Jn 20:24-27) confronted with doubts, sophistication, and indifference should handle belief as we deal with love. Just as fading love cannot be remedied solely by an intellectual approach, neither can a fading belief!

Get on your knees! In love accept the Lord Jesus as "the Way," and He will love you and reveal Himself to you (see Jn 14:21).

S the Father has loved Me [Jesus], so have I also loved you. Remain in My love. — Jn 15:9

DEC.
24

Abiding Love for Jesus

Jesus says, "I am the vine, and you are the branches. Remain in Me, as I remain in you" (Jn 15:5, 4). If spouses really love one another, they will be on one another's mind even when there is a temporary separation. In a way, they remain present to one another. Correspondence and long distance calls keep them united in love.

Apply this to your relationship with the Lord! How do you keep the line of communication open?

FOR this day in the city of David a Savior has been born for you Who is Christ the Lord.
— Lk 2:11

DEC. 25

The Mystery of Christ

This passage explains the mystery of Christ. "This day": God is present every day of the year. "In the city of David": Jesus is son of David, directing God's people of all ages, and indeed Messiah, i.e., Anointed King. "A Savior": He rescues us from alienation on both the human and the religious level. "Born for you": Christmas concerns me every day of the year. "Lord": Jesus transcends and rules over all people.

How to find Jesus? Pray for faith to accept Jesus gratefully and to see Him in others.

BEHOLD, the dwelling of God is with the human race.
—Rev 21:3

DEC. 26

The Lord's Presence

I am impressed when I see relatives' friends, and neighbors flock together around loved ones when death has struck in the family. In time of distress we don't want to be alone. The Bible says God Himself will be with us. He will wipe every tear from our eyes (Rev 21:3-4). This will be fully realized in the hereafter. But even now we can experience God's loving presence during time of pain if in faith we just open up.

Are you aware of God as one of the family? We are never alone. "Lord, enhance my awareness of Your loving presence!"

188

UCH was the appearance of the likeness of the glory of the Lord.

— Ezek 1:28

The Glory of God

Ezekiel describes the absolute majesty of God in a vision conditioned by his time and culture. A storm wind, huge clouds with flashing fire, figures sparkling with gleam like burnished bronze, the rainbow, a firmament like glittering crystal, and a throne on which God having the appearance of a man is seated are the figures of speech (see Ezek 1).

Could a walk in nature give you an awareness of God's greatness? Try it! "Ascribe to the Lord . . . glory and praise" (Ps 29:1).

E [the Lord] said . . . , "Fill your stomach with the scroll I am giving you." So I ate it, and it tasted sweet.

— Ezek 3:3

Assimilating God's Word

In a realistic way, the prophet Ezekiel indicates that we should assimilate God's word in the scroll (Bible) like food and be aware of it as "sweet." In other words, "Take to heart all the words that I speak to you. Listen to them carefully" (Ezek 3:10).

How much time do you spend on taking in junk (cheap TV shows and novels), and how much on assimilating meaningful fare, God's word included? Pray, "You are My refuge and My shield; I hope in Your word" (Ps 119:114).

YET I will remember the Covenant I made with you in the days of your youth. — Ezek 16:60

DEC. 29

Fidelity to the Covenant

Is growing stale the fate of all relationships? Unquestionably, there are couples who grow old graciously. Ezekiel refers to our youthful love for God and the process of aging.

What about your relationships on the horizontal level; spouse, friends? Any unanswered letters? As for your life of love with your Maker, Who is also your Spouse (see Isa 54:5), are you growing older graciously? Remembering your conduct and being ashamed? (see Ezek 16:61). "I confess. . . ."

DRY bones, hear the word of the Lord! —Ezek 37:4

DEC. 30

Renewal in God

Apathy may cripple both our personal and our collective relationships with God. That's why our Church, God's people with the hierarchical office as service to the disciples, needs reform constantly. Ezekiel's vision conveys a lesson. In our Church one may observe "How dry they are!" Can these bones come to life? God says, "I will bring spirit into you, and you will come to life" (Ezek 37:3-6).

Vatican Council II has started the much needed revival of our Church. Be with it! Don't be a dry bone yourself—and pray, "Come, Holy Spirit, and enkindle in us the fire of Your love."

190

AY [God] give you the spirit of wisdom and revelation so that you may know Him better.— Eph 1:17

The Spirit of Wisdom

A sense of direction and the motivation to keep moving is the secret of a happy Christian. It is a wisdom of life that results in a "knowledge of God," which in Biblical idiom is richly qualified by intimate love. It is a gift, a revelation, that God gives and must continue giving us.

Hence, meditative openness and constant growth in love-knowledge of God, in Whom we live and move, is the key to a happy life. "God, send Your Spirit of Wisdom and help me grow in love-knowledge of You!"

God's Living Word
in the Bible

Seek the Lord while He may be found,
    call upon Him while He is near.
Let the wicked man forsake his way,
    and the unjust man his thoughts.
Let him appeal to the Lord to have mercy on
    him.
    and to our God, Who is bountiful in forgiving.

For My thoughts are not your thoughts,
    neither are your ways My ways, says the
    Lord.
As the heavens are exalted above the earth.
    so are My ways exalted above your ways,
    and My thoughts above your thoughts.

Indeed, both the rain and the snow
    come down from the heavens,
but they do not return there
    until they have watered the earth,
    making it fruitful and productive,
giving seed to the sower,
    and bread to the eater.

That is how it shall be with My word
    that goes forth from My mouth.
It shall not return to Me void,
    but shall do whatever I wish,
    achieving the end for which I sent it.

Isa 55:6-11